TEA IN CHINA

TEA IN CHINA

THE HISTORY OF CHINA'S NATIONAL DRINK

JOHN C. EVANS

Contributions to the Study of World History, Number 33

Greenwood Press
New York • Westport, Connecticut • London

Library of Congress Cataloging-in-Publication Data

Evans, John C.
    Tea in China : the history of China's national drink / John C.
Evans.
        p.   cm.— (Contributions to the study of world history,
    ISSN 0885-9159 ; no. 33)
    Includes bibliographical references and index.
    ISBN 0-313-28049-5 (alk. paper)
    1. Tea—China—History.   2. China—Social life and customs.
I. Title.   II. Series.
GT2907.C6E93   1992
394.1'2—dc20   91-23428

British Library Cataloguing in Publication Data is available.

Library of Congress Catalog Card Number: 91-23428
ISBN: 0-313-28049-5
ISSN: 0885-9159

First published in 1992

Greenwood Press, 88 Post Road West, Westport, CT 06881
An imprint of Greenwood Publishing Group, Inc.

Printed in the United States of America

The paper used in this book complies with the
Permanent Paper Standard issued by the National
Information Standards Organization (Z39.48–1984).

10 9 8 7 6 5 4 3 2 1

To
Jack and Evelyn

Contents

Acknowledgments

I owe a great debt of gratitude to the following people who enthusiastically gave of their time to assist me in many ways: H. H. Albert Chung Sze, son of the last imperial ambassador to the Court of St. James who, despite failing eyesight, read and commented on the text; H. H. the Maharani Seeta Devi Gaekwar of Baroda who sparked my interest in tea years ago and so often invited me to afternoon tea served from the solid gold Baroda teaset; Baron Paul Pourbaix who provided me with several invaluable books; Mr. Robert Dick, supervisor, U.S. Board of Tea Examiners, who kindly replied to my many questions that must surely have tried his patience; Dr. Ptak, professor, Heidelberg University, who provided me with an extensive bibliography that proved so valuable; and Mr. Sam Twining, director, Twining's Tea Company, who personally took time to answer several pointed questions.

Special thanks are due to my principal translator, Li Kwan, who not only spent hours pouring over Chinese texts but also showed typical Chinese initiative and used an extensive invisible network of family ties and relations (*guanxi wang*) to procure texts he thought would interest me.

Although they are too numerous to mention individually, I owe a debt to my many tea-friends in China, India, Europe, and the United States whose comments and criticisms all helped in one way or another in shaping this book.

Chinese Dynasties

Shang	1766–1123 B.C.
Zhou	1124–222 B.C.
Qin	221–207 B.C.
Han	A.D. 206–220
Three Kingdoms (Wei, Shu, Wu)	220–280
Six Dynasties	420–588
Sui	581–618
Tang	618–907
Five Dynasties	907–979
Song	960–1126
Yuan (Mongol)	1271–1368
Ming	1368–1644
Qing (Manchu)	1644–1912

Note on the Text

Any transliteration of Chinese characters is arbitrary at best; this was made even more confusing when the old-style Wade-Giles spelling was replaced in 1979 by the *pinyin* spelling. *Peking* became *Beijing*, for example, but how many will recognize *Guangzhou* as *Canton*? In order to keep up with the times, the *pinyin* spelling is used throughout this book except where clarity and reading ease require old-style spellings.

Teamen call individual tea groves "gardens"; here they are called "plantations." The term "garden-tea" is used in its original sense to mean tea cultivated in the plains as opposed to "hill-tea," which, as the name implies, is grown on hillsides or mountains.

Some readers may appreciate the use of the seventeenth-century English vernacular "china cup" to designate handleless Chinese tea bowls.

1

Once Upon a Time . . .

Piercing China's secrets has never been easy, even for Chinese historians. Forgotten millennia shroud China's proud past in mystery. Tea is among the world's oldest beverages and, like most Chinese discoveries, its invention is so ancient that the original discovery can no longer be traced. Even the ancient Chinese had lost track of tea's true advent and were forced to imagine its beginnings.

The first Chinese were awed by the physical world surrounding them that so totally escaped their control. They spent hours pondering their universe, passing on to their descendents an overpowering urge to explain the existence of things. Attempts to account for events beyond their understanding gave rise to elaborate creation stories that became an integral part of early man's religion. These are our myths and legends.

Voices speaking from ages past, myths and legends have been handed down from generation to generation. Although they are inadmissible as historical evidence, myths and legends do have historical importance because they provide the only account of tea's origin. Because they form part of our cultural heritage, it is our duty to pass them on to future generations.

Once upon a time King Shen Nong, known as the father of agriculture and medicine, decreed that for health reasons his subjects must boil water before drinking it. One day as Shen Nong sat in the shade of a tea tree boiling water, a light breeze blew some of the tea leaves into the kettle of boiling water; when he drank the infusion he marveled at its delicious taste and at once felt invigorated. Tea had been invented. King Shen Nong is purported to have recommended it to his subjects, saying, "Tea gives vigor to the body, contentment to the mind, and determination of purpose."[1]

Although the famous ninth-century Tea Master Lu Yu affirms that tea was discovered by Shen Nong,[2] a king named Shen Nong probably never lived. In China's remote past *Shennong* was the name of a primitive farming tribe. One clever, unnamed Shennong chieftain is said to have invented plowing tools and discovered medicinal herbs, including tea, through personal experimentation.[3] For lack of a better tradition, legend has accorded him the status of a divinity, the name King Shen Nong, and the title Father of Tea.

Imaginative souls trying to add credence to the legend have even advanced the date of 2737 B.C.[4] as the year of tea's discovery by Shen Nong. Another date of 2690 B.C. has also been advanced.[5] How fortunate it would be had the advent of tea been so precisely detailed and dated, but such is definitely not the case. Any attempt to try to date tea's first appearance could be off by tens of thousands of years. Chinese historians have wisely disclaimed such futile speculation, contenting themselves with the neat, catchall tag "ancient."

Precisely dating the Shen Nong legend is no longer possible, but it is important to point out that when the first written texts mentioned tea they were based on a much older oral tradition. This fact proves that the use of tea was already ancient by the time of the first literary references to it. Shortly we will show that boiling drinking water was one of prehistoric man's earliest discoveries, a discovery made in the Stone Age 500,000 years before Shen Nong is supposed to have lived.

Tea no doubt made early men feel invigorated, but neither they nor any Shen Nong could have "marveled at its delicious taste," since early tea's taste was, as we will see, so bitter as to be hardly palatable.

The Shen Nong legend contains just enough plausible suppositions to sound credible. It is the most generally accepted tea origin myth. But matters were later complicated by the appearance of other legends challenging Shen Nong's discovery of tea. One of these legends spread throughout the Orient, traveling wherever tea and Buddhism went, and it gained a large following in Japan. This Buddhist version of tea's discovery is important because of its central importance to Zen Buddhist religious practice.

Once upon a time an Indian named Prince Siddhartha Gautama made a pilgrimage to China and to prove his faith he vowed never to sleep, not even for years. Misfortune befell him one day when, overcome by fatigue, he fell into a deep sleep. Upon awakening Prince Siddhartha was so ashamed and angry at having broken his vow that he tore off his eyelids and cast them on the ground, where miraculously they took root. From them suddenly sprouted a bush of shiny green tea leaves. Eating these leaves alleviated Prince Siddhartha's weariness and so aided his meditation, or *zen*[6] that he recommended tea to his followers.[7]

Chinese histories confirm that "during the reign of Emperor Xuan WuDi the Venerable Bodhidharma came to Northern Wei from southern India to teach Buddhism."[8] However, it is interesting to note the absence of the least mention of tea in relation to Siddhartha by Chinese historians. This silence is quite revealing.

The Siddhartha legend formed the basis of the ritualistic tea ceremony formalized during the Song Dynasty that was exported to Japan, where the meditative Zen Buddhist tea ceremony *chanoyu* survives today. The association of tea and religion was so closely bound that the Japanese word for both "eyelid" and "tea" is the same.[9] Apart from its obvious religious importance, the Siddhartha legend took on major historical significance in the nineteenth century when it was advanced as "proof" that tea had originated in India, a perfect illustration of a modern myth.

Tea is indigenous to both China and India,[10] so which country can claim to be the birthplace of tea? The debate for an Indian or a Chinese origin for tea began in Berlin in 1889[11] and raged for over fifty years until after World War II, when conclusive proof was presented. Despite good judgement and sound reasoning, there are some who would continue the debate today.

According to Indian tea origin theorists, tea was taken to China by Prince Siddhartha in 519 B.C. This presumption is clearly unfounded because tea had been part of the Chinese pharmacopoeia for at least one thousand years before Prince Siddhartha's birth. Diehards of the Indian tea origin theory hold that it was not Prince Siddhartha who brought tea to China anyway, but rather a Chinese traveler to India named Gan Lu. He supposedly returned to China with Indian tea plants that he planted in China's Sichuan province. Here again the Gan Yu theory fails to convince because, like Siddhartha, Gan Lu was born long after tea had come into widespread use in China.

A single false supposition can be used to fabricate an entire theory that is wholly erroneous. The "evidence" presented by the Siddhartha and Gan Lu legends rests on a foundation of quicksand. Although the Chinese historian Bai Shouyi believes that "ancient myths and legends reflect the historical reality of primitive society,"[12] it is best to heed the Greek historian Arrian's wise advice to "not inquire too closely where ancient legends about the gods are concerned because many things which reason rejects acquire some color of probability once you bring a god into the story."[13]

Putting aside all myths and legends, what are the facts permitting us to determine whether tea originated in India or China?

First, ancient Chinese texts mention tea by name several times but scholars scrutinizing early Indian texts have not found a single reference to tea. In fact, there is not even a Sanskrit word for tea, and the modern Hindi name for tea (*chai*) actually derives from the Chinese *cha*.[14]

Unlike China, there are no traces of any ancient tea cultivation in India. Of course, the British under the aegis of the East India Company transformed India into a great tea producer in the nineteenth century with over a million tea plants *imported from China* (see Chapter 11). Later, Indian tea plants were transplanted in Indonesia and in the African possessions of the British but *never was a single tea plant imported into China*.

An Indian tea origin cannot be supported by any historical fact and certainly not by legends. Ironically, the more "evidence" diehards produce in an effort to prove that tea originated in India, the stronger the case for a Chinese origin appears.

Furthermore, Indian tea origin theories began to circulate—no doubt by a concerted design—at just the time when the British were most anxious to sell the Empire Tea grown in their colonial possessions. Crowning India the "Birthplace of Tea" naturally added prestige to Indian teas and provided a very good selling point. In this light Indian tea origin theories flagrantly appear for what they are, namely, a British commercial ploy. Voltaire once remarked that if a lie is told often enough, people will believe it.

It is unquestioned historical fact that tea was first cultivated in China.[15] Thus, the Middle Kingdom is the undisputed birthplace of tea, from where it began the meteoric rise culminating in its becoming the world's most popular beverage.[16]

NOTES

1. Curt Maronde, *Rund um den Tee* (Frankfurt am Main: Fischer Taschenbuch Verlag GmbH., 1973), 16–17.

2. Lu Yu, *The Classic of Tea*, trans. Francis Ross Carpenter (Boston: Little-Brown, 1974), 115.

3. Bai Shouyi, ed., *An Outline History of China* (Beijing: Foreign Languages Press, 1982), 55.

4. L. Patrick Loyle, *The World Encyclopedia of Food* (London: Frances Pinter, 1982), 674.

5. Maronde, *Rund*, 17. I have been unable to trace the exact origin of these dates although I suspect they have come from German sources (Dr. Kämpfer?) via Japan. What seems more plausible is that quite possibly a zero was lost in translation for a date of 27,370 B.C. and 26,900 B.C. during China's Ancient Tribal Period.

6. *Zen* is derived from the Sanskrit *dhyana*, meaning literally "he thinks" and in a larger sense "meditation." The Chinese is *chan*.

7. J. Rambosson, *Histoire et légendes des plantes utiles et curieuses* (Paris: Librairie de Firmin-Didot et Cie, Imprimeurs de l'Institut, 1881), 307–308.

8. Bai Shouyi, *Outline History*, 195.

9. Inge Ubenauf, *Vom höchsten Genuß des Teetrinkers* (Niedernhausen: Falken Verlag GmbH., 1983), 15. The German reads, "daß im Japanischen Wort und Schriftzeichen für Augenlid und Tee ein und dasselbe sind."

10. Eelco Hesse, *Tee* (Munich: Gräfe und Unzer, 1985), 11.

11. Aleíjos, *T'u Ch'uan, grüne Wunderdroge Tee* (Vienna: Wilhelm Braumüller, Universitäts-Verlagsbuchhandlung GmbH., 1987), 23. Pages 23–28 of this very interesting book treat the subject of the "Urheimat des Teestrauches."

12. Bai Shouyi, *Outline History*, 57.

13. A. de Sélincourt, *Arrian's Campaigns of Alexander* (London: Penguin Classics, 1971), 225.

14. Ibid., 25. The German reads, "daß in Sanskrit für *Tee* kein Zeichen existiert." Note the use of *Zeichen* and not *Wort*.

15. Ibid., 28. The German reads, "daß der Tee erstmalig in China angebaut worden ist."

16. After water.

2

All the Tea in Sichuan

THE PREHISTORIC PERIOD: c. 1,700,000–c. 1600 B.C.

Legends are far more alluring than truth, which may explain why they arose and why we are so fond of retelling them. Despite romantic longing, however, tea's advent cannot be ascribed to a king, prince, priest, or scholar. The highly civilized Chinese who lived five thousand years ago did not know—nor will we ever know—the true circumstances of tea's discovery. Although it is impossible to ascribe a date to man's discovery of tea, archeological finds have revealed that it was more ancient than has previously been supposed. In all likelihood the first to discover some utility in tea leaves was neither king nor prince, but rather the brutish ape-like ancestor of modern man.

The first Chinese was Yuanmou Man, who lived about 1,700,000 B.C. More ape than man, Yuanmou Man is a difficult ancestor to venerate and his short stature proves he was not of the legendary race of "human giants" from which Chinese legends say their race descends.

During the 1930s Professor von Königswald bought hundreds of "dragon teeth" in Chinese pharmacies. These proved to come from neither dragons nor a race of superhuman Chinese ancestors, but from the extinct *Gigantopithecus blacki*, the largest primate that ever lived. Larger than any gorilla with an estimated height of at least ten feet, this primate is the fabled Tibetean *yeti*, Hollywood's "abominable snowman," and the North American "Bigfoot." Examination of the dragon teeth sold in Canton pharmacies until as late as the 1960s reveals that *Gigantopithecus* was a vegetarian whose diet consisted of fruit, leaves, grasses, nuts, berries, roots, and vegetables.[1] This huge creature's natural habitat was the primordial forest where tea grew wild, and it is probable that *Gigantopithecus* ate tea leaves as he roamed through the wilderness, actually discovering tea before man did.

Between A.D. 265 and 290 the following story was recorded in *The Supplement to the Collected Records of the Spirits*:

> A man named Qin Qing wished to go into the mountains to collect some tea. During one visit there he encountered a man covered with hair and over ten feet tall. He led Qin down the mountain, pointed to a tea tree ready for harvesting, then he departed. But he shortly reappeared and pulled an orange from his bosom and left it for Qing. Terrified Qing seized his tea, threw it over his shoulder and ran away.[2]

Had *Gigantopithecus* survived to the historic period, or is the story a fragment of the collective memory of a lost time when primitive man and his giant primate cousin coexisted? Maybe Richard Wagner was referring to a similar situation when he wrote: "Kräuter und Wurzeln findet ein jeder sich Selbst,/ Wir lernten's im Walde vom Tier."[3]

If Yuanmou Man consumed tea at all, he would have done as *Gigantopithecus* and eaten wild tea leaves. Prehistoric man's life was an exhausting one wrought with dangers, and most did not reach the age of fifteen. Under these conditions the need for a mind and body stimulant can be easily understood. Chewing tea leaves was one way to counter fatigue and restore the physical strength required for foraging for food over miles of undulating steppes. American colonists in the eighteenth century chewed tea leaves to alleviate physical and mental fatigue, and today Australian aborigines chew the leaves of the *Leptospermum*, nicknamed the "tea tree," whose leaves are used as a substitute for tea. Inhabitants of India, Africa, and the West Indies chew on caffeine-containing cola nuts for their stimulating effect.[4]

According to the Buddhist tea origin legend, Prince Siddhartha "ate" tea leaves to remain mentally alert. Had an earlier tea origin legend reflecting a time when tea leaves were chewed as a stimulant been retained and adapted by Buddhists? The concordance of man's first presumed use of tea and one of tea's oldest origin legends seems too great to be a mere coincidence.

The history of man living so long ago is difficult to reconstruct and traces of tea use are harder still to find. We only know with certitude that the primeval forest of Yunnan where Yuanmou Man lived is the home of tea, placing the first known Chinese in a region where tea was present in abundance.

Millennia ago a prime evolutionary lesson was demonstrated when the more intelligent human ancestor and not his muscled cousin *Gigantopithecus blacki* best adapted to the environment and survived.

The next link in man's evolutionary chain was *Homo erectus pekinensis*, the famous Peking Man[5] appearing 500,000 years ago who, although stooped, walked and ran erect. Still possessing some primitive primate features, he was nonetheless a human; it would not be facetious to say he resembled a heavy-set, brutish modern man.

Peking Man remained culturally at the Stone Age level, yet his manual dexterity, inventiveness, great industry, and innate sense of the grandiose make him appear already utterly Chinese in character. He was able to preserve, control, and use fire. In the cave dwelling Peking Man called home at Zhoukoudian outside modern Beijing is the largest hearth ever made by man with an ash level twenty feet deep. This astounding firepit ranks in scale with the Great Wall, the Qin Emperor's Tomb, and the Grand (Imperial) Canal. The enormous hearth radiated ample heat for Peking Man's comfort while the flickering flames frightened away any dangerous animals. He also used the great firepit to roast animal meat and boil drinking water.[6] (Boiling water to purify it had been among man's earliest discoveries, and even today the Chinese prefer to drink "healthy" warm water.)

It is Peking Man's intriguing firepit that provides a clue to his possible tea drinking. Archeologists know he had not yet learned the vital secret of making fire and was consequently forced to keep one burning all the time. The cutting, hauling, and stockpiling of the awesome amounts of wood consumed in the firepit demonstrate Peking Man's great industry. We know from ancient texts that early man in the historic period felled tea trees before picking the leaves.[7] Peking Man may well have done this, using the tea tree's branches and trunk for firewood while boiling its leaves in the drinking water with other plants to make herbal teas.

No evidence other than the boiling of water and the availability of tea leaves permits us to assume that Peking Man actually consumed tea in liquid form. Peking Man's sturdy lower jaw and the wear and tear on his teeth, which prove he was an omnivore, show that he did a considerably greater amount of chewing than modern man. He may have only chewed stimulating tea leaves for hours while he gathered food in the forest or while he chopped down, cut up, and hauled the tea tree logs back to his cave to be used as firewood.

Skeptics doubting that Peking Man (and by extrapolation Lantian Man or even Yuanmou Man) used tea have underestimated early man's natural botanic expertise. Paracelsus said that "All fields and alpine meadows, all hills and mountains are pharmacies."[8] Early man's very survival depended on his ability to distinguish harmful from beneficial plants, to discern which were nourishing and which were healing. Exceptionally acute olfactory powers enabled him to detect the scent of game on a wisp of air, perceive the various healthful minerals in a handful of soil, and sniff the goodness of plants. Invigorating tea would no doubt have been part of primitive man's pharmacopoeia.

The great firepits of Peking Man disappeared with him as a new species appeared to reign as master of the earth—*Homo sapiens*, the "Thinking Man," ourselves. Appearing in remote antiquity 40,000 years ago, our ancestors knew how to make fire and no longer needed to keep one burning constantly. This was an achievement of no mean proportions, because in order to make a fire a man had to reason. Reasoning led to writing, and the written record man left of his passage on earth became the essence of history.

THE HISTORIC PERIOD: BEGINNING 1600 B.C.

Wild tea trees reach maturity after four years, blossom with pretty white or pink blooms, and bear fruit in the form of oily, edible (distastefully bitter!) tea nuts. A glossy-leafed evergreen "sending forth its leaves even in winter,"[9] this member of the genus *Camellia*[10] (the so-called tea-family) can reach a height of over thirty feet.

The ancient Sichuanese felled tea trees before picking the leaves, as their ancestors no doubt had done for thousands of years. Cutting down a tree just to pick its leaves appears absurd at first glance but was actually quite purposeful. Tea harvestors armed first with stone axes, later with bronze and iron-bladed ones,[11] felled only tall mature tea trees, a selective weeding at once removing the old trees and making room for young ones. The trunk and branches of felled tea trees provided the firewood to boil the tea-water, so no part of the tea tree was wasted. Later, when the demand for tea increased, it was no longer possible to continue cutting trees—risking extinction—so cultivation was introduced and the old axe-wielding tea harvest was permanently abandoned.[12]

The ancient tea harvesting was seasonal, with spring being the most advantageous season because then the most fragrant, tender tea leaf buds appear in great number. In addition, the soft sap-saturated wood of the tea tree destined for firewood would have time during the hot summer weeks to dry out.

If the tea leaves were only gathered once a year, how were they preserved for the rest of the year? Would the Sichuanese mountain dwellers go outside in all kinds of weather and cut down a tea tree every time they wanted a cup of tea? These were questions early tea drinkers asked themselves when they faced the problem of storing and conserving tea.

One cannot eliminate the possibility that tea leaves were left out in the air and sun to dry (desiccate) like the logs of the tea tree itself, nor can it be excluded that even at this early date a form of airtight tea cake had been made. Until celestial food tea is discovered intact in the heredity jars of an ancient tomb, early man's most common method of making and conserving tea can be assumed to have been in liquid form.

At the beginning of the historic age tea was consumed in a liquid form that bore little resemblance to modern tea. Several caldrons and three-legged bronze pitchers existing from this early time furnish a wealth of information about early Chinese bronze casting and artistic tastes, but they provide no clues for determining the temperature and time used to prepare early tea. Was it made by decoction (*ao*), a long high-temperature boiling; by simmering (*yang*); or simply by boiling in a large amount of water (*zhu*)? Any modern casserole dish can be used in as many ways, while its shape and the material from which it is made afford no clue as to how it is used. The first literary mentions of tea all agree that its taste was remarkably bitter; from this we can infer that tea had undergone a rather lengthy brewing if not indeed a lengthy stewing.

Every cook knows that extended boiling reduces liquids. Early Sichuanese tea drinkers no doubt allowed tea to stew for hours, evaporating much of the liquid to result in a tea concentrate. Stored in sealed earthenware jars, this tea concentrate could be kept indefinitely. Whenever tea was required a part of the tea concentrate would be measured out and boiling water in prescribed amounts added to it. Tea concentrate is actually an ancient version of instant tea. It could be made once a year during the spring harvest and was readily available and easy to prepare throughout the rest of the year. Even in modern times tea concentrate remained the traditional tea of several Chinese mountain peoples and the boatmen plying the Grand (Imperial) Canal.[13]

Perhaps because heavy, cumbersome jars of tea concentrate were difficult to transport tea remained a strictly local commodity, produced and consumed within the narrow confines of its birthplace in Sichuan. At least as late as the Zhou Dynasty (c. mid-eleventh to eighth centuries B.C.), tea had only just begun to be used outside the remote mountainous region of its discovery.[14]

Water constitutes more than 50 percent of a fresh tea leaf, and during brewing this "bitter water" was infused out of the leaves. (All early writers commented on this characteristic bitterness.) Tea's bitterness provides an important clue permitting the assumption that early tea drinkers decocted freshly picked tea leaves.

Ancient tea's bitter taste is well known but its aspect remains mysterious, since allusions comparing it to "liquid jade" are the only extant descriptions of ancient tea's appearance. An innate Chinese fondness for jade developed at the very beginning of Chinese civilization and each succeeding dynasty has highly prized it. Jade comes in several colors varying greatly in shade, and each has enjoyed fashion's favor at one time or another. The best way to know which color and shade of jade was in style during a particular era is to observe the color of period ceramics made in imitation of it. Archeological excavations on a massive, unprecedented scale since 1949 have revealed the perfection of early ceramics made to resemble precious jade. Exquisite Shang Dynasty (1766–1123 B.C.) pottery was decorated with a light green glaze similar to pale green *piaoci* porcelain. Tastes changed with the times and during the Zhou Dynasty (1124 B.C.–222 B.C.) the preferred jade color was a rich dark green. These glazes serve as a reference indicating the color of the "liquid jade" early Chinese writers had in mind when they compared tea to jade.[15]

It is significant that every extant reference to ancient tea's appearance indicates that only *green* tea was made. This excludes the possibility of an ancient origin for black tea, which the Chinese call "red" tea.

Coarsely picked tea leaves and stems were brewed along with many other plants that were not intended for flavoring (even though early tea's bitter taste certainly would have benefited from it) but that were selected for their organ-specific qualities. Ancient formulas could be quite involved, calling for as many as forty or more different plants for a single cup. Today China's United Pharmaceutical Manufactory Fushan markets a throat-soothing Kam Wo Tea (Chu Kiang Brand) based on an ancient formula containing thirty-one different Chinese herbs.

Tea leaves were also used to make an ointment applied topically to relieve rheumatism. In the *Pillow Book of Cures and Prescriptions* a remedy for chronic skin ulcers calls for mixing bitter tea and centipedes. These should be "roasted until sweet and cooked until disintegrated. Then pounded and strained and boiled into a soup mixed with sweet herbs. Wash the sores and apply the decoction."[16]

Early tea was exclusively a medicinal plant belonging to China's vast herbal pharmacy. Ever since times of remote antiquity, tea's stimulating effects (due to caffeine) had earned tea its medical mark of approval. It is tempting to consider the possibility that if tea had not possessed a medical reputation the beverage we know today might never have existed.[17] The Sichuanese began drinking tea without other plant additives[18] only after village settlements appeared. Apparently tea was considered a digestive drink to relieve the heavy feeling caused by a diet of prodigious quantities of meat. Today tea is still recommended for people eating large amounts of meat.

Tea was a far cry in this early stage of its development from the delicious modern social drink. Recently wild tea trees were discovered in the primeval forests near Nanchuan in Sichuan. Tea from these wild trees would certainly taste like the first tea drunk thousands of years ago—a taste very different from modern tea, which is the product of centuries of selective cross-breeding.

The Zhou Dynasty was an epoch marred by continuous strife and upheavals, a period that was nonetheless conducive to creativity. Among the notable inventions of the Zhou were chopsticks. The instability and insecurity of the time provided fertile ground for the rooting of China's three great philosophy-religions, which were of capital importance in the spread of tea in China. The rising popularity of Taoism, Buddhism, and Confucianism paralleled the increasing popularity of tea as converts to each religion waxed into a great body of tea drinkers. All three would leave an indelible imprint on Chinese tea customs, many of which can be traced back to the Zhou Dynasty.

The first to coalesce in the quagmire of the Zhou Dynasty's death throes was Taoism, derived from the Chinese word *Dao*, literally "Universal Law" or more commonly "The Way." Founded by Laozi (born c. 604 B.C.), Taoism is a philosophy of simplicity and harmony appealing to the great masses; it later proved to be a counterweight to the Confucianist code of morality of the ruling classes. Taoism became immensely popular with the peasant classes and most of the teamen in Sichuan became Taoists. A story often cited as "proof" that tea originated in Sichuan tells us that when Taoism's founder, Master Lao, made his famous Western Journey he was handed a cup of tea to "strengthen and refresh" him by a student at the Han Pass near Shong-tu-fu in Sichuan.[19] Although the veracity of this story can no longer be verified, its re-telling had a decisive influence on Chinese tea manners. Taoists always offered tea to visitors as a greeting gesture in remembrance of Master Lao, a custom that is now the mark of Chinese hospitality. In addition, because a student had handed tea to Laozi a precedent had been established; thereafter it became the duty of inferiors to serve tea to their betters. During the revolt of the Four Princes in the Qin Dynasty Emperor Hui Ti had to flee, but when he returned the eunuch

Lo Yang is said to have given him a cup of tea—the ultimate form of honor.[20]

The Buddhist belief that tea bushes sprouted from Prince Siddhartha's torn-off eyelids must, like any miracle, be accepted on faith. Buddhism in any case laid sacred claims on tea, which became central to the Buddhist religious practice—the tea ceremony—in the same way that wine is central to the Catholic Mass. Just as in the country of the Vatican there is a wine called *Lachryma Christi*, or "Christ's Tear," in Buddhist China there is a tea called *Sow Mee Cha*, or "Eyelid Tea." Devout Buddhists reverently presented offerings of tea to statues of Buddha always portrayed in the meditative posture. Offering Sacrificial Tea to Buddha was an obligation in Buddhist homes and monasteries and was formerly an imperial duty of Chinese emperors.

The famous contemporary of Prince Siddhartha was Kongfuzi (551 B.C.–479 B.C.), better known in the West by the Latin form of his name, Confucius. Master Kongfuzi formulated a code of ethics for the scholarly ruling classes that stressed duty and obedience. It so profoundly affected Chinese thinking that all aspects of Chinese life became subtly influenced by Confucianism.[21]

Whether Laozi or Siddhartha actually knew and used tea is speculative, but Confucius had to have tasted tea in order to write in the *Book of Odes* (*Shih Jing*), "Who can say tea [*tu*] is bitter? It is as sweet as the shepherd's purse [*tsi*]."[22] Another writer compared girls to the "flowering *tu*."[23]

Laozi, Siddhartha, and Konfuzi are remembered as devout, sober, travel-weary men. During their proselytizing wanderings tea stimulated their intellectual energy and refreshed their tired bodies. These founding philosophers intimately linked tea forever to China's religious lore.

Tea in Zhou China was still a largely unfamiliar entity and at this early time there was much confusion surrounding its name. The authoress Pau Ling Hui entitled a work "Fragrant *Ming*," another name for tea. By the end of the Zhou Dynasty in 222 B.C. tea was known by the various names *chuan*, *jia*, *ming*, *she*, and *tu*, reflecting the partition of China into feudal states with different calligraphic styles.[24] *She* was Sichuanese for tea,[25] while in the *Erh Ya* the Duke of Zhou said the word *jia* is used to denote tea when it is bitter.[26] In the commentary to this work by Kuo Pu, however, it is specified, "When the leaf is plucked early it is called *cha*, if taken later it is referred to as *ming* or *chuan*. The Sichuanese call it "bitter tea'."[27] Others held that "When tea has a sweet flavor it may be called *jia*. If it is less than sweet and of a bitter or strong taste it is called *chuan*. If it is bitter or strong when sipped but sweet when swallowed it is called *cha*."[28] Here is the first mention of the word *cha*, which became the accepted name for tea and still remains the word for tea in modern Chinese. Already in the *Ben Cao* the names *tu* and *cha* are used interchangeably.[29] The final preeminence of *cha* would be remarked in a seventh-century commentary on the *History of the Early Han* when Yen Shih-ku noted that at the time *cha* was preferred to *tu* place names also underwent a change and the *Tu* Ling Hills at the beginning of the Han Dynasty became the *Cha* Ling Hills.[30] These different names indicate that tea was already over a considerably wide area in China.

As tea spread farther into other provinces other names would appear— for example, *te* (pronounced like the *e* in p*e*t) in the Amoy district of Fujian province. This is the word from which the English "tea" derived. Louis LeComte writing in 1696 said that "name is *cha* everywhere but Fujian Province where it is called *té*.[31]

Notably absent from the early list of tea names is the modern Mandarin *cha*, formed when the older ideogram *tu* lost a stroke, a cross-bar.

TEA AND LACQUER

Chinese lacquer—called *daqi*, or "major lacquer"—is at least four thousand years old, and the rise of lacquer exactly parallels that of tea. It is quite possible that Sichuan lacquer makers were also the world's first tea drinkers since tea and lacquer both originated in the same mountainous region.

Lacquer was early recognized for its durability and resistance to moisture, acids, and alkalis while it was lightweight and attractive. In the Zhou Dynasty works *The Book of Feizi (Han Feizi)* and *Tribute of Yu (Yu Gong)*, the use of lacquer is noted for the first time in the manufacture of dining and sacrificial utensils, including the first tea tables. These are decorated with exquisite five-color red, yellow, blue, white, and black lacquer.

The discovery of Zhou Dynasty lacquer teaware and tea tables across China provides direct evidence that tea was already available and widely used throughout China before the Qin Dynasty unification.

NOTES

1. Jan Jelínek, ed., *Illustrated Encyclopedia of Prehistoric Man* (Paris: Gründ, 1978), Chapter 1.

2. Lu Yu, *The Classic of Tea*, trans. Francis Ross Carpenter (Boston: Little-Brown, 1974), 132.

3. Richard Wagner, *Parsifal* (Stuttgart: Philipp Reclam jun. GmbH. & Co., 1980), 50. "Herbs and roots each finds for himself, We've learnt that from the beasts in the forest." Used with permission.

4. Dr. Galen C. Bosley in a letter to me dated January 12, 1989. Caffeine is a naturally occurring substance of the xanthine family of stimulants and is found in at least sixty different plant species.

5. Jelínek, *Illustrated Encyclopedia*, 10–21. "Peking Man" is actually the fossil remains of more than forty males and females of various ages. Unfortunately, the entire collection of Peking Man's remains, which were so painstakingly gathered, was senselessly destroyed during the barbaric Japanese occupation of China prior to and during World War II. By sheer chance enough plaster castings and scientific papers had been safely sheltered in European and U.S. collections to enable anthropologists to reconstruct his way of life.

6. Bai Shouyi, ed., *An Outline History of China* (Beijing: Foreign Languages Press, 1982), 3.

7. Lu Yu, *Classic*, 132.

8. Ibid., 63. Paracelsus lived 1493–1541.

9. Ibid., 15.

10. The genus name for tea is adapted from *Camellus*, the Latinized name of the Jesuit priest Georg Josef Kamel who died in 1706.

11. Christopher Hibbert, *Les empereurs de Chine* (Paris: Éditions du Fanal, 1982), 28.

12. Ethne Clarke, *The Cup that Cheers* (London: The Reader's Digest Association, 1983), 6.

13. Aeneas Anderson, *Relation du voyage de Lord Macartney à la Chine*, ed. Giles Manceron (Paris: Éditions Aubier Montaigne, 1978), 67–68.

14. See Chapter 4, paragraphs 5–6.

15. Bai Shouyi, *Outline History*, 241. "Primitive celadon, a green porcelain, appeared as early as the Shang Dynasty."

16. Lu Yu, *Classic*, 142.

17. When tea was first imported into Europe in the seventeenth century it was toted as a medicine, becoming a social beverage only several decades later.

18. Curt Maronde, *Heißgeliebter Tee* (Niedernhausen: Falken-Verlag GmbH., 1981), 6.

19. Aleíjos, *T'u-ch'uan, grüne Wunderdroge Tee* (2d ed; Vienna: Wilhelm Braumüller, Universitäts-Verlagsbuchhandlung, GmbH., 1987), 31.

20. Lu Yu, *Classic*, 133.

21. Hibbert, *Les empereurs*, 18.

22. Lu Yu, *Classic*, 13. Shepherd's purse is the *Capsella bursa pastoris*.

23. Ibid., 12.

24. Ibid., 59.

25. Ibid., 123.

26. Ibid., 122.

27. Ibid., 132.

28. Ibid., 113.

29. Ibid., 141.

30. Ibid., 13.

31. Ibid., 37. The title of LeComte's two-volume work is *Nouveaux mémoires sur l'état de la Chine*.

3

Zhongguo
The Middle Kingdom

As Hannibal crossed the Alps with his elephants to attack Rome in 218 B.C., China was unified for the first time by the Qin. It was the Qin Dynasty (221–206 B.C.) that forged the Chinese nation and as a fitting, lasting memorial commemorating this brief important dynasty the name "China" derived from *Ch'in*, the old-style spelling of Qin.[1]

The army of life-size terracotta soldiers and horses excavated in the "Divine City" of Chang'an (present-day Xi'an in Shaanxi province) stood guard over the greatest tomb ever built for a single man, the Qin Tiger. He was the dynasty's founder, known as the Exalted First Emperor of Qin.[2] Like so many dream emperors the Qin Tiger squandered chests of gold and literally worked thousands to death in an effort to realize monumental building projects that included his own amazing tomb, the Great Wall, and a multitude of magnificent palaces. More than 700,000 peasants were conscripted to work on Efang Palace alone and the same number worked on the Great Wall.[3] These great building projects brought laborers and craftsmen from all parts of China together in the work-camp melting pot. Conversation was the only amusement, the only release from the drudgery of the task, and men spent hours talking of their homes, families, and the life they had left behind. Certainly they boasted about their mothers' and wives' home cooking while praising their regional dishes, which were surely delicious compared to the meager fare of Chinese cabbage, or *baicai*, that had been developed at this time expressly for the workers on the great building projects. However, no tea was allotted to the laborers, and those that had drunk it before being drafted into the work force certainly would have complained about the distressing lack of it. A homesick, exhausted worker might sigh, "Sure wish I had some tea to give me a boost." Men from other regions where tea was unknown would ask, "What's tea?" The surprised reply, "You don't know tea?" would be followed by an enthusiastic explanation. "Well, let me tell you . . ." Showing an eagerness to impart his knowledge he would say, "Back home we only bought Sichuan 'fragrant *she*' that makes you feel like an emperor!"

In the work camps there existed a Babylonian mixture of spoken dialects and a man listening to or simply overhearing this conversation might add, "This *she* you're talking about we call *jia* where I come from and believe me there's no better remedy for a heavy stomach." Another would have to say his piece as well, offering, "You country bumpkins don't know anything. In the town I hail from we call it *ming* and there's nothing better to insure long life."

Like all Asian countries, China is a land of whispering walls. There are no secrets anywhere and grapevine news is never to be underestimated. Beijing mandarins were often informed by their house-servants of an event happening three thousand miles away before they learned of it through official bureaucratic channels. Whispers across China were a permanent and potent source of information, and people would surely have learned about tea by word of mouth years before they had the occasion to taste any.

When the workers of the great Qin building projects returned to their native places many picked up some tea along the route to take home, in some cases sustaining themselves along the route by it. As the entire family gathered around, listening to exaggerated tales of life in the wider world, the worker would prepare a pot of the novel tea, explaining, "Here's the marvelous 'Elixir of Life' drunk by the Qin Tiger himself! It will chase all the evil internal heat like nothing else and keeps inevitable death away from the door for as long as possible." He was sure to relate one of the tea discovery legends he had heard in the work-camp to amuse his listeners as he brewed the tea. Who would not be spellbound and impressed?

Just as the three great religions of China spread by word of mouth, so did the knowledge of tea.

Unification of the country translated concretely into increased trade within China as internal communications were improved. Goods and men traveled farther and in greater numbers than at any time previously. Tea, which was already available across China, could now be obtained even more easily. A glib, ambulating merchant might tell a client, "Do you know the folks just five days' walk from here consume a miraculous herb called tea?" A housewife might reply, "Try and get some for us on your next trip 'round."

At this time the veracity of the ancient tea legends was surely doubted by many and yet another tea origin legend appeared. Once upon a time the wife of a poor scholar had no money to buy food so she cut the leaves and stems from an ornamental tea bush growing in their garden to make a soup. Divine discovery! Its taste and physical effects enthralled the scholar, who hit upon the idea of selling the tea leaves and made a fortune.[4]

Like all tea origin legends, this one has just enough logical semblance of truth to be credible. No longer is tea's discovery ascribed to godlike supernatural people; now it is ascribed to a scholar. It is necessary to point out that this legend bears a strong modern coloring, even an unfamiliarity with China that hints of a foreign origin. Scholars were the upper ruling class of feudal China, and although it was not impossible to find a poor scholar as a stock character in a novel, they were in reality rare. Furthermore, scholars never jeopardized their social position by engaging in trade that would have reduced them to the lowest merchant class. That tea was discovered by a woman does not accord at all with the Confucianist ideal in which women were subservient to men in all respects.

What is worth noting in the scholar tea discovery legend is the putting of both the "leaves and stems into a soup." Even today, Japanese "Branch Tea" is a mixture of both tea leaves and stems. Did a tea soup exist similar to (for example) sorrel soup? Evidence indicates that at this time tea soup may have been one of the regional variations of tea, perhaps born from the necessities imposed by a period of famine. Throughout Chinese history people ate bark and grasses stewed in boiling water during famines. It is not inconceivable that tea itself had been "discovered" in such a period, since it has been persistently believed that man can live on tea alone. The poorest backwoods American farm families in the nineteenth century drank the strongest cups of tea; it was said they existed solely on tea and corn meal. The bitterness of stewed tea leaves and stems would be countered by inexpensive flavoring additives such as onions and herbs, but unfortunately no recipes listing the ingredients of an early tea soup have survived.

Obscured across three thousand years, our knowledge of tea's early use is frustratingly fragmentary. As Livy observed, "the mists of antiquity cannot always be pierced." Fortunately, however, tea figured among health-giving plants; otherwise when Qin Shi Huanghi ordered all books burned save those treating medicine, pharmacology, and field and forest plants, the already scanty early historical record of tea would have been lost in the literary inferno.[5]

"First Emperor" Qin Shi Huanghi was a cruel, capable ruler suffering from megalomania and delusions of grandeur, paranoia, and a persistent fear of death. Throughout his life he drank potions purported to be miraculous elixirs of long life, one of which was a startling mixture of powdered jade and tea.[6] It was this half-crazed ruler who gave tea its imperial cachet.

Qin Shi Huanghi reflects in the extreme many of the characteristics of this nascent period that later came a typify Chinese civilization. One of these characteristics is the obsession with long life. Each of the three philosophy-religions (Taoism, Buddhism, and Confucianism) adopted the theme of longevity, institutionalizing the respect and obedience due old age in a cult of elders and ancestors. Taoists in particular became obsessed by long life and an Elixir of Life became a Taoist ideal. For Taoists the Elixir of Life was believed to be tea. To insure long life people swallowed special Eternal Life pills washed down with cups of Elixir of Life Tea. Most Sichuanese teamen were Taoists, which suggests the possibility of a commercial interest dictating the Taoist selection of tea as the Elixir of Life.

As "proof" to substantiate claims that tea was the Elixir of Life, it was generally believed that one could subsist only on tea. Many scholars and holy men were said to take no nourishment except for bowls of tea. This, of course, was a marvelous selling point in favor of tea. For centuries the holiest monks demonstrated their faith by living only on tea; that is, until the Yuan Dynasty when the fraud was discovered that these canting men had used tea-like shreds of meat instead of tea leaves.

Tea owed its rising popularity to its reputation as a health-preserving and life-lengthening tonic. Who could resist such claims? Skeptics had only to look at the sturdy, robust Sichuanese who had been tea drinkers for generations to be convinced of tea's salutary qualities.

The great change in the way tea was perceived during the Qin Dynasty accounts for its rising popularity: Medicinal tea had become tonic tea. To understand the difference, remember that medicines cure whereas tonics keep one fit. Chinese medicine had always stressed prevention; therefore, doctors recommended tea to healthy patients to keep them that way. Of course, the market for tonic tea destined for healthy people desirious of maintaining good health was far greater than that of medicinal tea solely meant for curing illnesses such as indigestion or rheumatism. It is precisely this change in attitude toward tea that marks the point of departure for its great rise in popularity and widespread use.[7]

Medical research has shown that the alkaloid caffeine[8] produced naturally in tea leaves stimulates the central nervous system, resulting in enhanced perception and awareness, accentuated mental prowess, and a rejuvenated feeling that chases fatigue. Tea has always been appreciated for the refreshing lift it gives, and if it did not actually physically rejuvenate people it nonetheless made them feel young. For this reason tea became associated with longevity. Moreover, medical researchers attribute the low incidence of cancer and heart disease among the Chinese in part to tea drinking, which makes tea a lifesaver, an Elixir of Life indeed.[9] All Chinese today will swear that tea is a long-life drink, a claim increasingly supported by modern medicine.[10]

During the Qin Dynasty tea had begun to enter the mainstream of Chinese life, available throughout what was then China. Many factors contributed to tea's spread, among them its likeness to magical jade, unification, religious beliefs, and massive building projects that brought different peoples together. The propagation of tea was noted by Chung Meng, who wrote in *Climbing the Tower in Chengdu* that "Aromatic tea [*tu*] superimposes the six passions and the taste for it reaches the nine districts."[11] The "nine districts" then composed the Middle Kingdom (*Zhongguo*), an area bordered by the Great Wall in the North and the Yangzi River in the South. Unification permitted greater trading within Zhongguo as well as with the surrounding states. These "barbarian lands" including Sichuan and Yunnan were not yet part of the Middle Kingdom, but they were precisely where most of the tea grew and were only later incorporated into the Celestial Empire.

As tea spread across the great expanse of China, tea customs took on individual characteristics resulting in varied regional differences that are present even today. These variations arose more from geographical isolation than from religious or ethnic differences. In some places tea remained a bitter medicine, in others it became a tonic Elixir of Longevity; some drank tea occasionally as a remedy while others drank great preventative quantities. Tea was chewed, stewed to make a soup, and decocted to make a drink. Depending on the remoteness of a locality many regional tea customs remained unchanged for a thousand years, surviving even to the present.

NOTES

1. Christopher Hibbert, *Les empereurs de Chine* (Paris: Éditions du Fanal, 1982), 39.

2. "Chin Shih-huang Ti Find," *Science Digest* 78 (October 1975): 13–14; "Super Tomb, Ch'in Shih Huang Ti," *Scientific American* 233 (September 1975): 54.

3. Bai Shouyi, ed., *An Outline History of China* (Beijing: Foreign Languages Press, 1982), 127.

4. E. J. Keall, E. Nagai-Berthrong, and John E. Vollner, *Catalog: "Silk Routes"—An Exhibition of East-West Trade* (Toronto: Royal Ontario Museum, 1983), 191.

5. Bai Shouyi, *Outline History*, 126, 167.

6. Hibbert, *Les empereurs*, 46.

7. "Tea as Medicine," *Science Digest* 69 (June 1971): 53–54.

8. Galen C. Bosley, "Caffeine: Is It So Harmless?" *Ministry Magazine* (August 1986): 26–28. In a letter to me on January 12, 1989, Dr. Bosley explained,

There are three compounds that come from plants and are considered xanthines or methyl-xanthine stimulants. These three compounds are theophylline, caffeine, and theobromine. All three are stimulants of the central nervous system, act as diuretics on the kidney, stimulate the cardiac muscle, and stimulate the smooth muscles of internal organs such as the intestinal tract and the bronchial airways. Theophylline is often used in asthmatics to reduce the bronchial constrictions to ease breathing. Of the three, theobromine has the lowest potency and is not used for medicinal purposes anymore. Caffeine is considered the most potent, although theophylline produces the most profound and potentially dangerous [effects] of the central nervous system stimulants. High intakes of tea containing theophylline have the same effect on the central nervous system as does caffeine. The use of either of these brings on symptoms of nervousness, restlessness, insomnia, tremors, hyperesthesia (profound sensitivity of the skin), and other signs of central nervous system stimulation. High doses can even cause seizures and convulsions. Theophylline has more of a potent effect on producing these symptoms than does caffeine. They produce a feeling of lack of fatigue even when fatigue is present. It is a deceptive chemical as to what is really occurring in the body.

9. It is a question of *green* China teas.

10. Curt Maronde, *Rund um den Tee* (Frankfurt am Main: Fischer Taschenbuch Verlag GmbH., 1973), 53–55.

11. Lu Yu, *The Classic of Tea*, trans. Francis Ross Carpenter (Boston: Little-Brown, 1974), 130.

4

The Great Han Dynasty
206 B.C.–A.D. 220

The Qin had paved the way for the Han Dynasty, ushering in a long peaceful reign of great artistic and scientific achievement. A decisive period in Chinese history, Han has come to symbolize "true China." Tea was to become inextricably bound to Han—Chinese—civilization.

The Han set to work at once to realize their imperial designs, implementing successfully a policy founded on commercial trading and territorial expansion. Han commerce reached a sophisticated level and their remarkably efficient trading system based uniquely on barter grew by leaps and bounds to finally encompass global trade. The Han Empire so overflowed with riches that the fabled capital Chang'an (Xi'an) passed into legend and two millennia later Han wealth and splendor were still recalled in the proverb, "The streets of Chang'an are strewn with money." A boon to tea sales, Han wealth translated into an increased tea-buying power that brought tea within reach of a greater, ever increasing number of Chinese consumers.

From a strictly historical standpoint the most important aspect of Han empire-building was territorial expansion. The "barbarian" lands outside the borders of Qin Zhongguo were annexed to the "Han country,"[1] and these provinces bear famous names synonymous with tea, namely, Fujian, Yunnan, and Sichuan. For the first time the birthplace and principal producer of tea, great Sichuan, was part of the Celestial Empire.

Annexation of the tea countries meant that tea was now produced within China, thereby making it "Chinese"; this new perception of tea was of vast significance. The introspective Chinese have always been wary and disdainful of anything "barbarian," which for centuries was the Chinese equivalent of "foreign." Tea produced in a barbarian land could be easily snobbed, but once these territories were incorporated into the Han Country tea became Han tea and any adverse stigmas were removed.

Furthermore, at this time the famous Zhandao plank road built along treacherous cliffsides shortened the distance between Sichuan and Shaanxi provinces, greatly facilitating the flow of people and goods, including tea. The prohibitive cost of transporting tea dropped because of the Zhandao Road, and as the price of tea dropped it became available to greater numbers.[2]

The tea trade was also greatly facilitated by a new way of manufacturing tea. In a court case a director of criminal justice during one of the periods of famine noted that Sichuanese women made "a gruel from tea which they were able to sell pounded into cakes."[3] This development of cake tea is of great importance in the propagation of tea, since tea in cake form was easy to transport and trade. Manufactures of cake tea developed and proliferated in Sichuan. A thriving cottage industry of single family exploitations came into being simply because cake tea was so easy to make.

Sichuan shined as the outstanding golden apple of the Han imperial harvest. Immense in both size and riches, Sichuan was an important source of copper and iron, of tea and lacquer. Giving an idea of Sichuan's riches at the time, the compilation *Records of the Historian* states that "a peasant owning two hundred acres of lacquer trees has a wealth equal to that of a marquis supported by one thousand families."[4]

Innumerable well-conserved, ancient lacquer objects remain from the Han Dynasty, among them lacquer ladles, vanity cases, pillows, and coffins. There are also tea trays, tea tables, and remarkably beautiful eared cups typical of the Han Dynasty. That these eared cups are found all over China in great numbers attests to the breadth of the Han trading empire. Eared cups are certainly among the earliest vessels used for tea and their high price surely made them worthy of tea. Inlaid with gold, silver, and copper, the eared *kouqi* cups such as those found at Mawangdui near Changsha were extremely expensive. Huan Kuan mentioned in *On Salt and Iron (Yan Tie Lun)* that "rich people use lacquer-ware with a silver mouth and gold ears, and gold and jade pots, while the middle class use hempen lacquer decorated with jade and *Shu* [Sichuan] cups decorated with gold. One decorated lacquer cup can be exchanged for ten copper ones."[5] The *Shu* cups are the teacups used in Sichuan, mentioned for the first time in history.

In addition to lacquer teaware, Han creativity can be seen in their proto-porcelain. Recent discoveries have revealed that bowl-shaped porcelain cups had served for tea as opposed to the common *zun* used for wine. Other teaware consisted of exquisite ceramic tea bowls that show a high degree of technical perfection.

At least as early as the Han Dynasty tea growers packed tea in lacquer chests that were sent around the Empire, actually killing two birds with one stone since lacquer and tea from Sichuan could be transported together. When tea exports were begun to Europe some sixteen centuries later, tea was packed for the ocean voyages into decorative lacquer tea chests that were manufactured using the same techniques as those current during the Han Dynasty.[6] These chests are now priceless museum pieces.

The taste of tea had not improved and remained very bitter. No flavoring additives are known to have been used to counter the bitter taste of tea because the bitter aftertaste was desired by the Han as the expected sign of a good tea.

Unfortunately, the term "liquid jade" or "jade green"[7] is the only clue to the appearance of Han Dynasty tea. At least at court the preferred jade was similar to the costly jade used to compose the extraordinary funerary suits of Prince Liu Sheng and Princess Han Dou Wan.[8] Han imperial jade was surely the same color and shade that the Han "liquid jade" tea was made to imitate.

Brand-name tea varieties undoubtedly existed but only traces of the ancient Han tea classification system are extant. Han tea drinkers were astute buyers, they were able to distinguish authentic from imitation tea and could differentiate between various grades of tea. The existence of name-teas shows how highly developed tea trading had become in the Han Country. The *Materia Medica* (*Ben Cao Jing*)[9] mentions "Yizhou Hills Tea," while other sources mention "Meng Mountain Tea." In a story entitled *Contract with a Slave* (*Tong Yue*), Wang Pao talks about buying "Wudu Mountain Tea."[10] Many more name-teas were undoubtedly known to Han tea buyers. All known Han name-teas bear the name of a famous mountain, showing that the Han took the proverb "Fine teas come from high mountains" literally. This also permits the assumption that no garden-tea was yet cultivated in China.

A certain snob value had already been attached to tea drinking. In the *Shih Zhou* it was related that a man wanted to refresh himself with some tea before crossing a river and asked some local people what kind of tea they had given him. Noticing the angry looks they gave him, he had to explain that all he really was asking was if the tea should be drunk hot or cold.[11]

Singularly absent from the list of Han name-teas are the flowery names given tea during later dynasties. The straightforward Han tea classification was based on a geographical nomenclature in which tea's quality was determined by the place where it had been grown. Season of harvest and leaf size were not yet part of this classification.

Human nature has changed little over the centuries, making it easy for modern man to imagine the sense of well-being the Han felt as they watched the vapors rising from their beautiful steaming cups of tea. These vapors were doubly soothing for the Han, who believed evil demons were chased away by the vapors. Good genii were found in the tea cups by Han medical men as well, since tea was listed in the *Materia Medica* as a medicine acting as "an antidote to herbal poisons, as a cure for swelling and abscesses in the head and as a sleep inhibitor." The famous Han surgeon Hua Tuo succinctly sums up the Han medical viewpoint (showing a marked Buddhist coloring) in his dissertation *On Food* (*Shi Lung*), "To drink bitter tea constantly makes one think better."[12]

Hua Tuo's use of the word "constantly" is significant because it shows that many Han by the end of the dynasty[13] were already drinking tea all day long, no doubt as a tonic of long life. Tea was not, however, a pleasant-tasting social beverage. That would come much later.

Tea drinking continued to spread widely and rapidly across the Han Country. People had begun to drink it throughout the day, setting the stage for tea's future rise to preeminence as the national drink of China.

Before leaving the Qin-Han Period it may be a good idea to examine an intriguing question: Did the Europeans of antiquity know tea? In order to answer this question properly a quick review of the important events in ancient trading will prove enlightening.

The Macedonian Alexander the Great conquered all the lands from Greece to the Indus River by 320 B.C., and he has the distinction of being the first European known to have reached the Far East. Alexander was still a long way from China, which was isolated from the rest of the world by the greatest ocean, the highest mountains, and the greatest desert on earth.

The fabled Land of the Seres was known to exist, yet it still remained an undiscovered mystery to the historian Arrian writing in approximately 130 B.C. In *Campaigns of Alexander* and *Indica* (*History of India*), Arrian states that the Phoenicians accompanying Alexander's expedition "for what they could make out of it" collected "precious plants along the way," but Chinese tea was not among them.[14]

After Alexander's death the Indian ruler Chandragupta and the Macedonian Seleucus I in 305 B.C. established a trading link, or "silk road," stretching from India to Macedonia. Seneca called this *commercium Serum*, or "commerce with the Chinese," meaning silk.[15] This accelerated commercial exchanges greatly and soon European demand for silk was so great that the Zhou and later Qin ordered peasants to pay taxes in silk in order to coerce them into producing more silk. At this time, however, China did not trade directly with Europe since all trade passed through the hands of Indian and Persian middlemen.

The Chinese knew as little about Europeans as Europeans did of the Chinese. As the volume of trade increased, Emperor Wu Di decided in 138 B.C. to send Zhang Qian on a mission to explore direct trade possibilities with the "western barbarian lands." Qian reported, "When I was in Daxia [Bactria, a city founded by the Greeks] I saw bamboo canes and cloth from China. When I asked how such articles came there people replied, 'Their merchants bought them in Yuandu [Shen-du, or India]'."[16]

Merchant ships regularly sailed from China's Guangdong and Guangxi provinces to India's Coromandel Coast and to other southeast Asian ports; from there goods were carried to the Middle East and Southern Europe.

It is worth remarking that Buddhist missionaries converted Ceylon at this time while other Buddhist monks arrived in Egypt, yet despite the importance of tea to their religion none of the monks reportedly drank tea. During the nineteenth century P. Colquhoun in his exhaustive treatise on the British Empire noted that in 1814 had been "found the real tea plant in the woods of Ceylon of a quality equal to any that ever grew in China."[17] Could this have been remnants of an ancient transplantation of tea plants in Sri Lanka?

A steady rise in silk exports to the West prompted the Han to send their emissary Gan Ying in A.D. 97 to Daqin (the Roman Empire) to try and break Parthia's (modern Iran's) monopoly of the silk trade.[18] The Parthians tried in every way to obstruct China's contacts with Daqin and even thwarted Gan Ying's embassy. The Romans themselves wanted to reach China to establish direct trading ties, and in A.D. 166 the ambassador of the Roman Emperor Marcus Aurelius Antonius arrived in China to return to Rome with silk, not tea. If he ever mentioned tea no record is extant.[19] However, detailed Roman roadmaps show with unexpected precision the route to China, dispelling any doubts as to where China was, but not even Imperial Rome at its height could sustain the cost of conquering, occupying, and maintaining such an extensive highway. Annual caravans of silk continued to go west to return laden with ivory, glass, linen, wool, carpets, glazed tiles, grape vines for wine, gold, and horses.[20] There was no demand for the unknown tea in the Roman Empire.[21]

It is easily misconceived that tea was among the articles China traded with Ancient Rome since there is a Latin name for tea. Tea's former genus name *Thea* (now Camellia) is indeed Latin—or more precisely New Latin, since it was only coined at the end of the seventeenth century by Dr. Engelbert Kämpfer and employed by Carl von Linné in his famous

Systema Naturae published in 1735. There was no Old Latin name for tea[22] and no trace of tea can be found on the detailed stocklists of the spices and herbs filling Rome's herb emporiums. Perhaps the Macedonians and Romans recoiled in horror when they encountered tea, for its liquid jade color was exactly the same as one of the most widely used poisons of antiquity—Cicero's dreaded *mortiferum poculum* of hemlock.

Tea is made with only water, therefore, good teas require good water. For this reason it is regrettable the Romans did not drink tea since they had an excellent water supply. Before the birth of Christ the Roman Curators of the Water Supply oversaw the building of great aqueducts to the hills miles from Rome. These brought an abundance of crystal clear mountain water gushing into the city's 700 public pools and 500 fountains.

The empire created by the Arab Conquests extended eastward to the borders of China forming a bridge—and trade monopoly—between China and Europe. During the Sui Dynasty (581–618) there were three trade routes to the West, all in the hands of the Arabs.[23] The Arab stranglehold on East-West trade pushed prices beyond the tolerable level, forcing furious Europeans to embark on a series of armed campaigns to try and break the Arab monopoly. Because these were launched in the guise of religion they are known as the Crusades.

Arab traders knew Tang Dynasty tea well, and one trader named Soliman even noted during the eleventh century that tea "cures all distempers."[24] History has shown that men would risk their lives to obtain tea. It has even changed the destiny of several countries, yet it remains a curious mystery why none of the tea so highly praised by Arab traders was carried West.

Only during Kublai Khan's reign is there proof tea had moved westward along the Silk Road, becoming the principal beverage in Balkh (Persia) but no farther. Europeans began to arrive in China at this time. Father Giovanni de Piano Carpini was sent by Pope Innocent IV in 1245; shortly thereafter in 1271 Marco Polo arrived, followed by Giovanni de Montecorvino in 1292. Their silence regarding tea is remarkable.[25]

The Silk Road had been open for centuries linking Europe to China but at no time was commercial tea taken in camel caravans or Arab dhows to Europe. The first tea to reach Europe arrived in small quantities on board European ships during the Late Ming Dynasty, and another century passed before any appreciable amounts were imported.

NOTES

1. Wou Tche-he, *L'art du thé*, trans. Nadine Normand (Taiwan: Éditions Philippe Picquier, 1990), 31.

2. Bai Shouyi, ed., *An Outline History of China* (Beijing: Foreign Languages Press, 1982), 165.

3. Lu Yu, *The Classic of Tea*, trans. Francis Ross Carpenter (Boston: Little-Brown, 1974), 126.

4. Cited in Pan Jixing, *Ancient China's Technology and Science* (Beijing: Foreign Language Press, 1983), 207.

5. Cited in ibid., 206.

6. J. R. ter Molen, *Het goede leven Thee* (Utrecht/Antwerp: Het Spectrum, 1979), 21, 28–29.

7. Lu Yu, *Classic*, 19.

8. Christopher Hibbert, *Les empereurs de Chine* (Paris: Éditions du Fanal, 1982), 19–27.

9. Ascribed to the "Creator of Tea" Shen Nong and often cited as *Emperor Shen Nong's Materia Medica*, the *Ben Cao Jing* is a work of the Eastern Han and is a prime example of the maddening Chinese habit of rewriting history. It contains 365 medicines, 252 medicinal herbs, 67 animal drugs, and 46 mineral drugs. The definitive edition is the *Compendium of Materia Medica* (*Ben Cao Gang Mu*), completed in 1578 by Li Shizhen. It contains 1,892 medicines and 11,000 prescriptions in 52 volumes. Charles Darwin quoted from this work.

10. Eelco Hesse, *Tee* (Munich: Gräfe und Unzer, 1982), 11.

11. Lu Yu, *Classic*, 132. It is remarkable in this citation that it is a question of drinking tea "hot or cold." Considering the Chinese aversion to cold water (because all water not boiled in China is unhealthy), I have nonetheless included it here since it would be the earliest mention of drinking "cold tea" in history if it is exact.

12. Ibid., 131.

13. Tche-he Wou, *L'art*, 22.

14. M. Annaeus Seneca, *Epistulae ad Lucilium*, ed. R. M. Grummere (Cambridge, MA: Loeb Classical Library, Harvard University Press, 1958), Ep. 00.13.

15. A. de Sélincourt, *Arrian's Campaigns of Alexander* (London: Penguin Classics, 1971), 332.

16. Bai Shouyi, *Outline History*, 141–142.

17. P. Colquhoun, *A Treatise on the Wealth, Power, and Resources of the British Empire in Every Quarter of the World* (London: Joseph Mawman, 1815), 411.

18. Bai Shouyi, *Outline History*, 155.

19. Ibid., 154–155.

20. John E. Vollner, E. J. Keall, and E. Nagai-Berthrong, *Silk Roads, China Ships: An Exhibition of East-West Trade* (Toronto: Royal Ontario Museum, 1983), 26–27 and 84–86. This outstanding exhibition toured in Canada and the United States through 1986.

21. W. S. Davis, *A Day in Old Rome* (Boston: Allyn & Bacon, 1950), 89. In a note to this page Dr. Davis adds, "About twenty years after the reign of Hadrian Chinese annals record that certain 'Roman' (Graeco-Levantine?) traders actually reached China, and gave themselves out as envoys to the 'Son of Heaven' from 'Antun' (Antonius Pius)."

22. E. Chatlain and L. Quicherat, *Dictionnaire latin* (Paris: Hachette, 1891), 1427.

23. Volner, Keall, and Nagai-Berthrong, *Silk Roads*, 26, 35.

24. J. Jumeau-Lafond, *Le thé* (Paris: Éditions Nathan, 1988), 11.

25. Bai Shouyi, *Outline History*, 321–322.

5

Feudal China
A.D. 220–618

Chinese dynasties followed a repeating pattern of forceful acquisition, accumulation of riches, and flourishing of the arts until a final burnout and precipitous decline. The great, unique Han Dynasty simply imploded in A.D. 220, collapsing under the weight of its own wealth and achievements.

When the Han Empire disintegrated all central power disappeared, leaving the unprotected population at the mercy of marauding bands brutally rampaging across the country. Terror reigned supreme in China. Order was only established after strongarm bandits carved out personal patchwork realms. Allegiance to these self-crowned sovereigns lasted only as long as they kept their heads. Treachery lurked everywhere.

A story from the Three Kingdoms Period (220–280) aptly portrays the instability and violence of the era. One of the self-proclaimed rulers named Sun Huo was a notorious drunkard who obliged every guest at his table to drink seven *shengs*, or quarts, of wine. The limit of his favorite, Wei Chao, was only three *shengs*, so secretly Wei Chao arranged with a friend to be given tea instead of wine. Unfortunately, the substitution was discovered and the enraged Sun Huo ordered Wei Chao (and no doubt the friend who had given him the tea as well) to be cast into a dungeon, horribly tortured, then executed in 273.[1]

Tea lovers traditionally style Wei Chao as the "Patron Saint of Tea," admitted by his martyrdom for tea into the Tea Pantheon alongside the "Father of Tea," Shen Nong.

The drunkenness of Sun Huo's court, where the punishment for sobriety was death reflects the alcoholic epidemic of the Three Kingdoms Period, a trend confirmed by the incredible number of period wine jars that have been unearthed.

As early as the Shang Dynasty different wines were brewed such as "sweet" rice wine or "fragrant" wine made from black millet. The many wine vessels discovered in the Yin ruins indicate that alcohol consumption was common among the nobility.[2] The well-known Chinese fondness for bacchanalian binges may have originated then as well, since wine was not sipped moderately but was gulped down as if taking the traditional Chinese toast ganbei, or "dry glass," literally. Several different alcohol-containing beverages may be served during a Chinese meal,[3] but never cold water or tea. The Chinese considered it unhealthy—even dangerous—to accompany a meal with tea, and for this reason warmed rice wine and bitter green wine were the preferred beverages of the Three Kingdoms Chinese. During this era so clouded with alcohol vapors a lonely voice of reason was heard when the writer Zhang Yi became the first to note that "tea sobers one after drinking alcohol,"[4] a comment adding a decidedly new twist to the general perception of tea. The exaggerated consumption of alcohol caused people of the Three Kingdoms Period to turn to tea to offset the effects of inebriation and to prevent the dreaded hangover. Tea had become a popular remedy for drunkenness and its ill effects.[5]

Everyone is familiar with the sobering power of a cup of coffee but few associate the same property with tea, although the sobering alkaloid caffeine is found in both. A cup of coffee contains twice as much caffeine as a cup of tea, making the sobering power of coffee doubly effective.[6]

Caffeine is produced naturally in a wide variety of plants including tea. Tea was certainly recognized at an early time as a "cure" for inebriation, and carousers in ancient China were given strong doses of green tea just as their staggering counterparts in Europe and America would be given strong cups of coffee. The diuretic properties of tea[7] were correctly observed to cause an increased elimination of body fluids, and the early Chinese mistakenly thought alcohol was eliminated by urination, thereby promoting sobriety (it was actually the result of caffeine's stimulation of the brain and an increased rate of oxidation).[8]

Bearing in mind that tea "cured" inebriation, the Shen Nong "discovery" of tea legend can be viewed in a new light. Stripping away the fabled mythic trappings, it is possible the "poison" for which tea proved to be the antidote was alcohol. Seventeenth-century Dutch Calvinists promoting temperance quoted from unnamed Chinese sources (the *Ben Cao Jing?*) echoing refrains popular in the Three Kingdoms Period when they advocated replacing poison alcohol by *sobering* tea.[9]

An abstemious trend developed over time and in roughly 370 Emperor Fu Jian Liang (who ruled 352–385) recommended "*sobering* tea" to his court, adding, "The precious liquid chases worry and gives a feeling of well-being."[10] During the reign of Emperor Xuan Wu Di (who ruled 499–515) in the Northern Wei Period, the abstemious trend was confirmed by the arrival of Siddhartha in China from South India to teach Buddhism and to found the Chan religion. The Buddhist emphasis on moderation and use of tea to aid meditation certainly accorded with the tempering times. The influence of religious movements has often proved decisive throughout history, and Siddhartha can be credited if not for beginning the abstemious current at least for encouraging it. The final word on the subject was voiced by the scholar Chin Mung in 560 when he praised tea as "better than wine because tea doesn't cause inebriation."[11]

However, not everything written about tea has been flattering and complimentary. Down through the ages tea has been the object of periodic animadversion and virulent attacks and even has been prohibited by law. Tea did not become the national drink of China without having its Chinese detractors.

The first recorded criticism of tea appeared (this is not surprising) during the intoxicated times of the Three Kingdoms. In his work bearing the awesome title *Collection of Wonders* (*Pu Wu Chi*), a writer named Zhang Hua listed tea under the chapter headed "Foods to be Avoided" because "drinking tea induces sleeplessness."[12] Another important writer in the history of tea, Zhang Yi, echoed this view: "Tea keeps one awake."[13]

The Han drank tea to "think better" and even if they reportedly sipped it "constantly" they nonetheless consumed it with moderation. During the Three Kingdoms Period, on the other hand, social restraints were relaxed and all drinks including tea were consumed immoderately, often abusively. Drinking too much tea too frequently may result in chronic sleeplessness (insomnia), a common fourth-century complaint providing indirect evidence that tea consumption was on the rise.

The Three Kingdoms Chinese customarily chased alcoholic beverages with tea. Considering the intemperance of the time, if great amounts of wine were matched with a proportional amount of tea it represented quantities sufficient to induce sleeplessness, a problem modern decaffeination has resolved.

In some parts of North China tea drinkers were insulted and disparaged for drinking tea. Northern Wei contempt for tea was such that it was recorded, "Tea is way off the mark and is the very slave of yoghurt."[14]

Tea's detractors were vociferous yet few and did not stem the rising popularity of tea.

People turned to tea not only as a cure for inebriation but also as a means of sustenance because severe droughts during the Three Kingdoms Period caused widespread famine. Whenever food was scarce people turned to tea. Sichuanese tea growers even introduced Rice Tea Cake, the first packaged meal made of large tea leaves (*souchong*) mixed with rice.[15] Rice Tea Cake made a tea soup that permitted thousands of famine-stricken peasant families to survive. The staple one-course tea soup could be enriched and flavored with herbs and hard-to-get vegetables or with a few precious shreds of dried meat. Tea was used in Chinese cooking during halcyon times as well, and such regional specialities as Sichuan's Camphor and Tea–Smoked Duck and Hangzhou's freshwater shrimp cooked in Longguing tea are famous delicacies today.[16]

The stimulating effects of tea were, of course, accentuated when it was taken on an empty stomach, and persons consuming it would have suffered chronic insomnia. A notable rise in tea consumption during lean and troubled times is often evident in history; poor people often "can't get to sleep" because they have drunk too much tea. Tea's high price deterred none because contrary to expectations those least able to afford tea have always drunk the strongest cups.

Information about the cultivation, harvesting, manufacture, packaging, transportation, marketing, and storage of tea up until the third century is scarce. Our knowledge of this early time comes from tidbits of information gleaned from many sources, including the "educated guess" and "negative evidence." Beginning in the third century, however, the tea historian stands on the firm ground of fact. At this time appeared the important *Enlarged Literary Expositor* (*Guang Ya*) written by Zhang Yi, which contains the first inestimable (far too brief!) description of ancient tea processing and preparation. It is with Zhang Yi that the literary history of tea in China begins, and in the Tea Pantheon he is undoubtedly the "Patron of Tea History."

Ancient, organized, highly productive tea cultivation was practiced in Sichuan exclusively by small one-family producers. Tea plants were laid out along strict, orderly delineations providing maximum efficiency; pruning was introduced to shape the tea plants into waist-high tea bushes bristling with easily picked tea leaves.[17]

When the demand for tea rose significantly in the third to fifth centuries, many new hill-tea plantations were created along the Yangzi River Valley following the course of the river, which was a natural, inexpensive highway to internal markets. In order to provide the thousands of tea plants required for the new plantations, great nurseries were organized and the reproduction of tea plants became almost as important a business as producing tea itself.

Tea leaves were always plucked by hand, by women, then as soon after picking as possible the fresh tea leaves were steamed in special on-site sheds. Steaming removed the "bitter water" from the fresh leaves and this important technical innovation resulted in a remarkable improvement in tea's taste.[18] (Here one is tempted to conjecture that had steaming not been developed or its development delayed for several critical centuries tea would not have become the national drink of China.) Wine was at this time the unquestioned national drink of China, and tea did not rival wine's preeminence until its taste had improved by steaming out the bitter water and it became viewed as a social drink. Improving tea's taste made it the right drink at the right time, fulfilling the need for a pleasant alternative to wine in tune with the temperance trend of the times.

Once the fresh tea leaves had been thoroughly steamed they were compressed into cakes. However, cake tea should not be mistaken for Yunnan *Beeng Cha*, or "compressed tea," marketed today because cake tea was as dense and solid as brick tea.

Han Dynasty consumers had been careful tea buyers, purchasing name-teas whose geographical origin represented a quality guarantee. Then as now, tea drinkers knew the young tender shoots (*pekoe*) made the best tea while older, larger leaves (*souchong*) were less desirable. The increasing complexity of the tea classification system reflects evolving tea tastes as well as the increased popularity of tea.

Zhang Yi found it necessary to give a detailed explanation on how to make tea. This indicates that tea's preparation was not familiar to all, due to a great number of new tea drinkers drinking a new style of tea. Zhang Yi's instructions to his contemporaries permit us to know exactly how tea in ancient China was prepared: "First bake the cake of tea until reddish in color then pound it into tiny pieces and put these into a porcelain pot. Pour boiling water over the leaves and add onion [actually, *pesai*], ginger and orange to flavor."[19]

Zhang Yi had given a recipe for hot spiced tea. No wonder there were so many new tea drinkers. A revolution had occurred and bitter medicinal tonic tea had been replaced by a pleasant-tasting beverage. The residents of the Yangzi River Valley are the first people cited as having "enjoyed tea."[20] Zhang Yi referred to tea as a "drink," not a medicine or tonic. Even the *Erh Ya*, a dictionary written in 350, defines tea as a "beverage," thus confirming its new social status.[21]

Ancient tea's agreeable spicy taste caused already rising tea sales to skyrocket during the Six Dynasties Period (420–588) when a tea craze swept across China.[22] Emperor Wu Di (ruled 482–494) so loved tea that he decreed that offerings of his favorite beverage be sacrificed to him after his death.[23] Zhan Qian Chi noted that the Emperor's tea came from Wen Mountain in Zhejiang province, half a continent away from its birthplace. Tea plantations continued to multiply to meet the ever-increasing demand of people now drinking tea for pleasure.

By the fifth century tea had become a big business. Sichuanese tea merchants amassed fabulous fortunes, while tribute tea revenues filled the Emperor's coffers with gold. A burgeoning retail market of brokers, dealers, and shopkeepers developed. Tea began to appear in taverns, wine shops, and noodle shops. Corollary trades such as ceramic and porcelain potters, lacquer and furniture makers, silversmiths and goldsmiths kept pace with the tea vogue by introducing expensive tea-things denoting status for people drinking convivial tea.

The years 590–618 correspond to the short-lived intermediary Sui Dynasty. Thousands of peasants were employed to dig a vast complex of waterways, including the Grand (Imperial) Canal that was highly instrumental in facilitating internal commerce. Within a decisive quarter century the Sui set the stage for the Tang, like the Qin who had paved the way for the Han and later the Yuan who cleared the path for the Ming. The Sui opened China's moongates for the glorious Tang Dynasty, beginning a golden age for tea in China.

NOTES

1. Eelco Hesse, *Tee: Die Welt des Tees und die Tees der Welt*, 4th ed. (Munich: Gräfe und Unzer, 1985), 11.

2. The Chinese only began drinking beer with meals in the nineteenth century after German breweries were built in China.

3. Including "Peking Shandy" made with orange soda pop and beer.

4. Zhang Binglun, *Ancient China's Technology and Science* (Beijing: Chinese Academy of Sciences, 1983), 332.

5. John Blofeld, *L'art chinois du thé*, trans. Josette Herbert (Paris: Dervy-Livres, 1986), 26.

6. Galen C. Bosley, "Caffeine: Is It So Harmless?" *Ministry Magazine* (August 1986): 26–28. It is possible to drink too much tea. The effects of too much caffeine are indistinguishable from anxiety neurosis.

7. The Chinese are constantly urinating from drinking too much tea. During the sit-in in Tienanmen Square in June 1989 the Red Cross, fearing an epidemic, wanted the demonstrators removed.

8. In the minutes of Volume 4 of the 10th International Medical Congress in Berlin in 1892 is an article by Emil Kräpelin entitled *Über alkohol und tee* comparing the effects of alcohol and tea on the brain.

9. In England the "Drink Tea!" campaigns of the 1740s launched by Fielding to combat gin abuse and the 1830s described by Dickens in the *Pickwick Papers* are famous examples of temperance through tea.

10. Aleíjos, *T' u-ch' uan, grüne Wunderdroge Tee* (Vienna: Wilhelm Braumüller Universitäts-Verlagsbuchhandlung, GmbH., 1987), 32.

11. Ibid., 32.

12. Ibid., 33.

13. Zhang Binglun, *Ancient China's*, 332.

14. W.F.J. Jenner, *Memories of Loyang* (Oxford: Clarendon Press, 1981), 215.

15. Aleíjos, *T' u-ch' uan*, 33.

16. Dan Gong, *Food and Drink in China* (Beijing: New World Press, 1986), 72. Longguing tea is customarily served in clear glasses as opposed to china cups so that tea-drinkers can enjoy the "wonderful color and movement of the fine tea leaves in the hot water" (Aleíjos, *T' u-ch' uan*, 36). Is this the origin of the Arab use of glasses for tea drinking?

17. Zhang, *Ancient China's*, 332.

18. Ibid.

19. Ibid.

20. Jean Runner, *Le thé* (2d ed.; Paris: Presses Universitaires de France, 1974), 14.

21. Lu Yu, *The Classic of Tea*, trans. Francis Ross Carpenter (Boston: Little-Brown, 1974), 122. For the past twenty centuries the Chinese have enjoyed tea as a social drink, yet curiously when tea was first imported to Europe it was considered strictly as a medicine. In France as late as the 1830s it was sold by apothecaries whose "Treatment Handbook" still listed tea as a medicine.

22. Horst Hammitzsch, *Zen in the Art of the Tea Ceremony* (New York: Avon Books, 1980), 26.

23. Hesse, *Die Welt*, 12.

6

Tang Dynasty
618–906

When the Roman Empire collapsed and Europe plunged into the Dark Ages the sun rose in the Orient with an extraordinary brilliance. The year 618 marked the founding of the Tang Dynasty and the beginning of a glorious golden age for China.

Chang'an was the capital of a flourishing empire of 53 million inhabitants living in ten *dao* (provinces). The extensive territorial limits of the Tang Empire roughly equalled those of present-day China.[1]

Luxury knew no bounds as the urbane Tang indulged their voracious appetite for all that was new and exotic. They began sitting on low lacquered furniture but etiquette allowed those who found this elevated position fearful to sit cross-legged as they had previously done on rugs. Servants wearing pointed caps served rare delicacies on silver, gilt, or jade plates during day-long sybaritic banquets. Grape wine was drunk from translucent jade cups.

Men's and women's closets were filled with long gowns embroidered with symbolic figures made of silk for summer and rich brocade velvet for the cooler winter months. Bright rainbow colors enlivened every gathering,[2] and the exotic national costumes of the large foreign population gave Chang'an a truly cosmopolitan appearance.[3] With the Tang had come "exotic products, music, dances, acrobatics, customs and religions."[4]

The Imperial Palace[5] comprised more than thirty large buildings set amidst sculptured pleasure gardens that included a polo field where boys disguised as women played the stylish new sport that had just been imported. The Hall of Mirrors hung with fabulous pearl curtains was a lavish setting for entertainment provided by actors, dancers, musicians, and acrobats as well as poetry readings and story telling. A game of chess called *wei ki* played with 360 pieces provided intellectual occupation for months.[6]

Scientific and technical innovations wrought lasting changes. Astronomy, mathematics, and medicine (notably acupuncture) developed dramatically during the mentally fertile Tang Dynasty. Cavities in teeth were filled with a silver paste for the first time. Printing with carved wooden blocks was invented. Libraries were required to house the encyclopedias that were compiled in an exhaustive effort to catalog the totality of human experience and knowledge.

Black and white landscapes by Wang Wei gave landscape painting its letters patent, while Tang poetry reached unsurpassed heights. The exceptional refinement characterizing Tang visual arts, ceramics, and especially poetry has earned the designation "Classical Age" for the civilization of the Tang Dynasty.[7]

Tang forcefulness and exuberance can be felt in the portraits of Tang emperors shown standing in flowing red gowns ready for action.[8] These rulers felt a special affinity with Taoism because they bore the same family name (Li) as its legendary founder (Laozi), whom they revered as their ancestor.[9] Therefore, it is not surprising that the Tang encouraged tea consumption. Tea drinking was popular at the time of the Tang accession but under them it became a passion. How fitting it was that the refined Tang should be the ones to elevate tea to a level of poetic sublimity.

TANG TEA CULTIVATION

The book *The Outline of the Four Seasons* (*Si Shi Zuan Yao*), which was probably the effort of several specialists working together, gives a detailed account of how and where Tang Dynasty teamen planted tea. In general, grafting was not practiced by planters; they preferred to raise new shoots from tea seeds. Once the tea seeds had been collected they were buried in sand until ripe, then transferred to a basket of moist pebbly soil. One year later the sprouts were bunch planted and intercropped with hemp, millet, and broomcorn.[10] Intercropping provided shade for the fragile young plants and helped to offset the planting costs accruing during the three unproductive years before the first tea harvest.

Tang tea cultivation was streamlined to a very efficient system permitting each cluster of tea seedlings to yield eight ounces of tea at maturity. Since one acre contained 840 clusters, total output of tea per acre was approximately 420 pounds, a high output. Today in Darjeeling about 570 pounds of tea are produced per acre.

Increased tea production became Tang state policy, and for the first time large government plantations appeared. During the Tang Dynasty tea was grown commercially in the present provinces of Anhui, Fujian, Guangdong, Henan, Hubei, Hunan, Jiangsu, Jiangzi, Shaanxi, Sichuan, Yunnan, and Zhejiang—and practically all the ancient Tang Dynasty tea plantations are still producing tea.

The ancient proverb "Famous teas come from high mountains" is as true now as it was in the Tang Dynasty. At that time the highly prized teas—Shihua of Mengding, Shisun of Guzhu, Luya of Fangshan, and Huangya of Huoshan—all came from high mountains. Often the small tea groves built around pagoda temples on inaccessible mountaintops tended by Buddhist monks produced the rarest—and consequently the most coveted and expensive—tea. Lu Yu stated that "tea growing wild is superior, garden tea takes second place."[11] In general, however, Tang tea cultivators planted hill-tea on shady land along mountain flanks subject to cloud cover, fogs, or frequent mists. When the large government garden-tea plantations proved successful there was impetus to plant newer, larger garden-tea plantations on low-level land not used to grow rice.

TANG TEA HARVESTING

Traditional tea harvesting followed stringent, invariable rules. All tea leaves were picked "prior to the spring rains" in March-April when new shoots (*pekoe*) had appeared and the leaves were young and tender.[12] Because tea leaves grow faster after the rains and are consequently larger, they are less desirable. Lu Yu warned, "One is likely to fall ill if tea is picked in the wrong season."[13] Tea from the spring harvest was named "Before the Rains Tea."[14]

As a general rule the warmer a growing region is, the sooner tea leaves there are picked. Cloudy or misty mornings are considered an especially favorable time to harvest tea leaves because then the leaves are most fragrant and moist.

All tea leaves were picked by hand, by young girls—according to legend only virgins (i.e., unmarried women)—who were said to be more dexterous and had a keener eye than others. They went in small groups into the tea plantations before dawn, their bodies clad in heavy quilted coats against the cold morning mountain air. Often, dense chilling fogs enveloped them and they were lost from sight, and were it not for their melodic singing no one would know they were there.

One of the beautiful old ballads sung by the tea pickers as they worked has come down to us:

> Up at dawn I push at my hair and dab at my face,
> Seize my basket and out the door while the mist lies thick.
> Young girls and those no longer so go hand in hand,
> They ask, "Which of Sunglo's peaks do we scale today?"
> Two by two one helps the other strip a branch.
> Each warns the other to not be slow,
> Because the buds on the branch are growing old,
> And the silky rain will fall tomorrow.[15]

Singing surely helped to relieve the tedium of the tea pickers' task but the girls always began to sing *before* they entered the tea groves and continued singing as they advanced through them as a precautionary measure to ward off the small poisonous vipers living in the tea bushes. Snakes posed a real threat, and the danger was further intensified because the optimum time for picking tea leaves was precisely when the sleeping vipers were most dangerous. Casualties each year could be quite numerous; due to the danger involved, young girls and unmarried older ones who were not considered as valuable as boys (because the dowry required to marry them off was an expensive burden) were employed for tea picking. Once a girl's family had paid a dowry she no longer picked tea leaves, because if she were bitten by a snake and died her dowry was lost. The ballad mentions "those no longer young" who also picked tea. These were widows and women past childbearing age whose utility to an ancient society was viewed as diminished.

Pickers had to keep their hands extremely clean and special attention was given each picker's fingernails lest they be too long or too short, because the fingernails—not the fingers—did the plucking. Body oils, perspiration, and body heat were thus kept from contaminating the fresh tea leaves. As a special precaution a "second skin" of silk gloves was sometimes worn; this covered the hands and fingers completely, exposing only the fingernails thrust through tiny slits in the tips. Attached to a belt around each girl's waist was a small jug of water that enabled her to wash her fingernails frequently. Pickers were forbidden to eat garlic, onions, or strong spices.[16]

The tea pickers put the leaves in large wicker baskets allowing easy access for the cool, moist morning air. As if this were not enough of a safeguard of the tea leaves' freshness, other girls stood in the fields manning large buckets of cold water with which they refreshed the tea leaves.

The day's harvesting always stopped before the sun had risen too high, usually before noon,[17] although occasionally it would continue longer if the sky was cloudy. The rest of the day was spent processing the morning's harvest, work done by men.

In the eighteenth century a story began circulating in Europe that Chinese tea harvesters threw rocks at monkeys and thereby so angered them that they ripped off branches from the tea trees and threw them on the ground, where teamen had only to bend over to collect them. Considering the extreme care taken by Tang Dynasty tea pickers to insure the freshness of the tea leaves it is inconceivable that the hands of a monkey would be allowed to contaminate any tea leaves, much less those grown especially for the Emperor's personal use. The Chinese practiced cliffside planting by means of "rappeling," i.e., using cords and ropes attached to the bodies of humans. Seen from a distance these planters might have looked like monkeys, whence a probable origin for the legend.[18]

In the famous Qing Dynasty novel by Hsueh-chin Tsao, *A Dream of Red Mansions* (also called *A Dream of the Red Chamber*), young maids served a "tea with such a pure scent and exquisite flavor called 'Thousand Red Flowers in One Cavern Tea'." People who read about this marvelous tea actually asked tea merchants for the same, not realizing it was the pure fantasy of a dream.

The monkey tea harvest story as well as legendary teas, porcelain, and other tall tea-tales should only be taken for what they are, namely, fables meant to amaze or amuse. A teahouse story-teller would never admit this, of course.

TANG TEA MANUFACTURE

When the fresh leaves were brought in they were first steamed and then crushed to form a paste to which plum juice—a natural glue—was added. The tea paste was poured into molds and compressed to form cakes that were perforated, strung together, and baked until dry. Brick tea, which was made the same way but in a different shape, appeared at this time for the export market.

Tea is easily spoiled by moisture, heat, bright light, microbes, and strong odors, but once the tea had been made into cakes or bricks no air or light could impair it. Practically imperishable, cakes and bricks of tea were so solidly compressed that it was impossible to scrape off the tiniest bit of tea with the fingernails. Another advantage of cakes and bricks of tea was that they could be easily accounted for and their number accurately recorded on a court official's abacus, thereby minimizing theft and tax cheating.

Cakes and bricks also facilitated transportation, stimulating southern tea sales in North China and outside the Empire.

Tea merchants' profits were so great that the *fei qian*, or "flying money," bill of exchange was invented to make it easier for them to bank their fortunes.

A thriving inter-province and inter-Asian tea trade developed. At its height the Tang Empire had established ties with Korea, Japan, India, Pakistan, Afghanistan, and even Iran and Arabia.[19] The "Hermit Kingdom" of Korea became a large market for Tang cake tea. This tea was also exported to the "Island of the Dwarfs" (*Jihpen-kwe*), or Japan.[20] A Buddhist monk named Diashi is supposed to have taken tea seeds hidden under his gown to Japan in 810 since the island ruler Saga so liked China tea.[21]

TANG DYNASTY TEA

Throughout the Tang Dynasty tea was prepared in various ways in various places. Even different classes of Tang society, rich and poor, urban and peasant, as well as foreign ethnics drank tea differently. The example of the Imperial Court set the standard for Tang tea drinkers, yet the influence of the Court was directly proportional to one's nearness to it. The expression "Tang Tea" of course refers to the tea that was fashionable at Court, either *tuan cha* or *yen cha*. These teas were familiar to scholars who left a literary record.[22]

As in previous dynasties, solid Tang cake tea was readied in the traditional manner by roasting the cake of tea until it softened and then pulverizing it with a mortar and pestle. In addition to the mortar and pestle various scrapers, knives, strainers, and a total of twenty-four tea implements were required. Most of these were made of bamboo or, for those who could afford it, bronze, silver, and gold—although Tea Masters did not approve of the use of metal tea implements.[23]

Since water is the only ingredient besides tea leaves in a cup of tea, Tang Dynasty teamen realized the importance of having a good quality water. A bad tea made with good water remains a bad tea, but a good tea infused in bad water is also bad. Today as in ancient times a good cup of tea depends upon the quality of the water as much as the quality of the tea.[24] At a time when good teas cost their weight in silver and gold no one dared to risk spoiling even a thimble cupful of tea with bad water, so great care was taken to insure that tea-water was pure. Lu Yu listed selected tea-water sources and chose mountain spring water over all others. Water from famous springs was "bottled" in earthenware jars and transported at great cost across China to be used in making tea for the Tang enthusiasts.[25]

Of course, expensive pure tea-water could not be wasted by contaminating it with "dirty fire," so Tang tea drinkers were advised to boil tea-water over a charcoal fire rather than one made of wood because its fumes were considered the least noxious. Even the temperature of the fire was closely controlled because only tea-water "boiling furiously" was considered proper for infusing tea leaves.[26]

The most popular tea drunk during the Tang Dynasty was made from "coarse, loose, powdered or cake tea. It can be chopped, boiled, roasted and then put into a bottle or pottery vessel where it awaits only hot water."[27] To this was added "sweet onions, ginger, jujube fruit, orange peels, dogwood berries, cloves or peppermint,"[28] making a hot spice tea we might call Tang Dynasty Tea. Lu Yu was harshly critical of spice tea, which he saw as "no more than the swill of the gutters and ditches."[29] This was a purist's judgement. Mulled Tang Dynasty Tea was the most common tea and it was no doubt delicious—hence its popularity. The hot spice teas drunk today recall the pleasing taste of Tang Dynasty Tea. Tea purists still frown upon hot spice teas but, as in the Tang Dynasty, that does not diminish their popularity. Lu Yu himself believed that the "goodness of tea is a decision for the mouth to make,"[30] which remains the tea drinker's golden rule.

In parts of China, however, the sweet spices were left out and only salt was added. This flavored slightly the tea whose bitter aftertaste was appreciated like "good advice."

The Tang improved tea cultivation and processing but their principal contribution lay in the realm of tea manners, for it was they who elevated tea to an ethereal level. Although tea was still considered a healthy drink and often qualified as "invigorating," it had now become a prestigious social drink, the national drink of China.

Large red hand-delivered invitations were distributed inviting people to the first tea parties in history. Tang tea parties were lively gatherings of friends and convivial occasions to have a good time. Even if the tea parties were often boisterous, a strict etiquette governed them. Servants had to hand teacups to guests with both hands to show respect and the host always drank before the guests, thus reassuring them the tea had not been poisoned. A guest had to conform to customary courtesy as well and every polite guest complimented the host by saying, "This is indeed good tea" even if its quality or taste met general disapproval, which was rare. Decorum might not be observed at all times but a proverb held that "Murder can be forgiven but insulting someone at tea, never!"

Hong Sheng's drama, the *Palace of Eternal Youth*,[31] contains a marvelous tea story illustrating the refined Tang sense of humor: Following in the Emperor's procession[32] were the beautiful duchesses of Qin, Guo, and Han, who were known to drop all sorts of things along the roadside whenever they passed. Peasants searching in the grass after the duchesses' passage found a gold hairpin with a ruby on it, an embroidered slipper with a pearl on it, and a gold box wrapped in a silk handkerchief containing sweet-smelling thin brown slices of a food thought at first to be a love potion. Two common women tasted it but straightaway spit it out, complaining with disgust, "It's bitter! How can people eat this?" Only the box and silk wrapping were kept and the priceless scented Imperial Tea was discarded.

Aside from showing the wealth and waste of the Tang, this story certainly amused courtiers who laughed at uncouth common women incapable of appreciating—or even recognizing—the finest tea in the Empire worth more than the gold box and silk wrapping containing it.

Social pressure was keen because the Tang high-life tea vogue and one's prestige depended on having the best cups of tea. Anyone suffering a dishonorable lack of tea knowledge considered themselves so shamed that they could only save face by removing their silk belts and hanging themselves from the nearest peach tree. Such an occurrence was rare, however, for surely everyone strove to acquire the stylish tea culture required for social success. Even more important than mere social standing was Lu Yu's warning that "Tea improperly prepared can cause sickness."[33] For this reason in the Tang Dynasty only those who knew how to prepare tea properly were allowed to do so.

The expertise needed to make tea gave rise to a professional class of Tea Masters, men who devoted their entire lives solely to tea. Some highly paid Tea Masters were employed by the Emperor and the powerful mandarins, others were in a single family's service, but in all cases the Tea Masters made sure their employers had the best and rarest teas, procured the purest mountain spring tea-water brought from sources across the Empire, and bought costly "smokeless" charcoal. Tea Masters experimented for weeks on end to get the right combination of tea, tea-water, and charcoal to make the perfect cup of tea. In addition, they made sure that all tea implements were of the best quality, including the highly esteemed blue glazed teacups, and always impeccably clean.

The need for an experienced Tea Master can be easily understood in light of the list of tea implements required to make a cup of Tang Dynasty tea. A professional Tea Master owned a carry-all made of bamboo in which slats divided the space into triangular and square cubbyholes for all the tea implements. The carry-all itself was deceptively small and it was amazing to see all that it could contain: a brazier; basket; stoker; fire tongs;

cauldron; stand; pincers; a sack made from thick white rattan; a roller made of orange tree wood or pear tree wood; gauze and casket strainers made of fine silk stretched over strong bamboo; seashell measures of the clam or oyster; a water dispenser made from the wood of the pagado tree covered with sewn cloth or lacquer large enough to contain ten pints; a "raw copper" water filter; a gourd water ladle; peach, willow, grape, or palm wood tongs one foot long with silver set into the ends; a stoneware salt dish four inches in diameter; a heating basin; a tea bowl made of Yueh porcelainware having a "greenish hue that enhances the true color of tea" with a lip that does not curl over holding less than eight ounces; a basket for cups; a brush of twisted strips of coir palm (*Trachycarpus excelsa*) bark set in a block of dogwood (*Cornus officinalis*); an eight-pint scouring box; a four-pint container for dregs; two cloths of course thread two feet long for cleaning the tea equipage; and a utensil rack of wood or bamboo to hold the tea implements in their proper order.[34]

In households boasting a famous Tea Master guests assisted at the preparation of tea, complimenting their host profusely (never the Tea Master directly) on the good quality of his tea and the refinement of his mansion. Guests often left the Tea Master a gift of money—"tea money," or tip—to show their appreciation on leaving.

Having a Tea Master avoided the waste of tea from handling it badly, which carried a loss-of-face onus. That was one of the three "most deplorable acts in the world along with false education of youth and an uninformed admiration of fine paintings."[35]

One of the most important duties of the Tea Masters was to select the costly teas packed into fine silver or gold boxes wrapped in silk that were presented as marriage gifts. The value of these presents reflected the giver's wealth as well as refinement.

The splendor of tea in the Tang Dynasty can be felt in light of the physical, mental, and social pleasure it afforded Tang men and women. "The first cup of tea," said Lu Yu, "should have a haunting flavor, strange and lasting. When you drink tea, sip only otherwise you will dissipate the flavor. Moderation is the very essence of tea. Tea does not lend itself to extravagance."[36]

As early as the Qin Dynasty Chang Meng-yan observed that tea "super- imposes the six passions," but it was the Tang poet Lu Tung who, living the life of a hermit near a freshwater spring like so many "tea-crazy" men, wrote what has become a tea lover's creed. Although exerpted from a larger work,[37] this oft-quoted stanza is traditionally called "The Seven Cups of Tea" and it aptly shows the sublime sentiments tea imparted to the Tang:

The First Cup of Tea moistens my Lips and Throat.
The Second Cup breaks my Loneliness.
The Third Cup penetrates my barren Entrails.
The Fourth Cup raises a slight Perspiration,
All the Wrongs of Life pass through my Pores.
With the Fifth cup I am purified.
The Sixth Cup calls me up to the Realm of Immortals.
The Seventh Cup is the Last—
I can drink no more.
Oh! I ride a Sweet Breeze and waft away.[38]

Peace, harmony, and well-being were felt when the Tang drank the "divine drink." Indeed, they considered tea to be literally divine since it represented the fulfillment of the Taoist ideal. For centuries an Elixir of Immortality had been sought that would release man from gravity's restraint and insure his eternal life. No doubt the *Dao shi* (Taoist priests) of the Tang Dynasty viewed tea as the prophesied elixir, enabling them to "ride Sweet Breezes to the Realm of Immortals."[39]

The harmony of the Empire was shattered when a series of rebellions began to fatally rock the Tang Dynasty. To finance the army a direct tax payable in copper money was imposed, then in 780 the imperial government levied an indirect tax on salt, wine, and tea—the first tea tax in history. Tea was an immensely profitable crop and a good source from which to replenish the Emperor's empty strongboxes. Three years after the first tea tax was imposed all private trading in tea was outlawed and tea became the personal monopoly of the Emperor.

Throughout the turbulent years of revolt Sichuan remained untouched by the civil strife, becoming a haven for exiles fleeing Chang'an and peasants driven off their lands. The massive influx of peasants seeking security and rich tea profits became known as Sichuan's Tea Rush, which was every bit as convulsive as California's Gold Rush. The flourishing tea culture that would bloom in the Song Dynasty was due in large measure to those peasants who had sought refuge in Sichuan, where they became expert teamen.

NOTES

1. Bai Shouyi, ed., *An Outline History of China* (Beijing: Foreign Languages Press, 1982), 210.

2. Ainslie T. Embree, ed., *Encyclopedia of Asian History* (New York: Charles Scribner's Sons, 1988), 67.

3. The Shah of Persia lived in Chang'an after being deposed during the Arab Conquest. Mosques and Nestorian Christian churches stood alongside pagoda temples in Chang'an *fangs* (city blocks). In Guangzhou (Canton) a period mosque contains the tomb of one of the Prophet's uncles. Mohammed was interested in Chinese culture and said, "Though China is far away, we should go there in quest of knowledge" (Bai Shouyi, *Outline History*, 217).

4. Ibid., 215.

5. Actually three palaces, namely, Taiji, Daming, and Xingqing Palaces.

6. John Blofeld, *L'art chinois du thé*, trans. Josette Herbert (Paris: Dervy-Livres, 1986), 22.

7. Edmund Capon, *Tang China: Vision and Splendour of a Golden Age* (London: MacDonald Orbis, 1989), 107–108.

8. Chiang Fu-tsung, *Masterpieces of Chinese Portrait Painting in the National Palace Museum* (Taipei: National Palace Museum, 1971), 11–16.

9. Denis Twitchett and Arthur F. Wright, *Perspectives on the T'ang* (New Haven: Yale University Press, 1973), 265.

10. Hemp was cultivated for its fiber used for cordage; millet, a kind of grass, was grown for its grain used for fodder; and broomcorn, a sorghum, was used for making brooms and brushes. Later, Indian corn imported from America would be used for intercropping.

11. Lu Yu, *The Classic of Tea*, trans. Francis Ross Carpenter (Boston: Little, Brown, 1974), 70.

12. Ibid., 60.

13. Ibid., 61.

14. Ibid., 22.

15. Ibid., 22–23.

16. Blofeld, *L'art*, 35.

17. Blofeld, *L'art*, 27.

18. Aeneas Anderson accompanied Lord Macartney to China in 1793 and brought this story home with him, although he admitted he had not seen the monkey tea harvest himself. See Chapter 10, 121–122.

19. Bai Shouyi, *Outline History*, 214.

20. The English "Japan" derives from Chinese; the Japanese say "Nippon."

21. Mariarosa Schiaffino, *L'heure du thé* (Paris: Gentlemen Éditeur, 1987), 14. Regrettably, the original Chinese tea plants taken to Japan have suffered from repeated cross-breeding. This has resulted in the inexplicable "fishy" taste of most Japanese tea, which is vastly overpriced.

22. Horst Hammitzsch, *Zen in the Art of the Tea Ceremony* (New York: Avon Books, 1980), 26.

23. Blofeld, *L'art*, 36.

24. Victorian teamen blended teas to match the water in particular parts of London. Now in Paris when one buys costly teas from the fine *traiteurs* in the Place de la Madeleine they advise using bottled Volvic water. Marianne Nicolin in *Tee für Genießer* (Niedernhausen: Falken-Verlag, GmbH., 1974; 24–28) lists the hardness of the tap water of 250 German, Austrian, and Swiss cities so that tea-drinkers there may buy appropriate teas.

25. Lu Yu, *Classic*, 105.

26. Ibid., 107.

27. Ibid., 116.

28. Ibid. Jujube is an edible fruit of the buckthorn family.

29. Ibid.

30. Ibid., 74.

31. Written in 1688.

32. Chiang Fu-tsung, *Masterpieces*, 45– 46. The pomp and circumstance of an Imperial Procession can be seen in this vivid illustration.

33. Lu Yu, *Classic*, 61.

34. Ibid., 77–79.

35. Ibid., 17.

36. Ibid., 111.

37. Blofeld, *L'art*, 29–30 gives the complete five stanzas of the "Song of Tea."

38. T. C. Lai, *At the Chinese Table* (Hong Kong: Oxford University Press, 1984), 36.

39. Bai Shouyi, *Outline History*, 219. In one of his edicts Li Shimin explicitly said that Taoist priests and nuns should be given priority over Buddhist monks and nuns. The Tang-Taoist-Tea triangle marrying religion and commerce helps to explain the social and political factors contributing to tea's immense popularity in the Tang Dynasty. Lu Yu's *Classic of Tea* had been written primarily to increase tea consumption and tea sales as part of Tang state policy. The case for the Tang-Taoist-Tea triangle is a strong one, although one must not lose sight of the fact that tea's popularity was due in large part to its pleasing taste.

7

Song Dynasty
960–1279

Unlike the foreign, cosmopolitan Tang, the introspective Chinese Song sought a return to traditional Chinese values.[1] Yearning for a civilization as perfect as the fabled Celestial Empire of their Han ancestors, the Song Dynasty was to be a nostalgic romantic age in Chinese history. Despite constant glancing over their shoulders to the idealized, unattainable centuries past, the Song nonetheless made great advances. In medicine they invented the smallpox vaccination (in 1014, almost 800 years before the Europeans), and in mechanics they invented the astronomical clock.[2] Their *huojian*, or "fire arrow," was the first use of gunpowder in war.

Poets described the Song capital Lin-an[3] (present-day Hangzhou), an impressive metropolis of multistoried buildings, as "sweet." Certainly the balmy, agreeable climate was conducive to enjoying life, befitting the Song quest for the good life. Undoubtedly they enjoyed life a little too fully, because drunkenness became such a problem that the government had to put balustrades around the canals to keep staggering, intoxicated pedestrians from falling in.[4] Bordering the capital was the famous *Xi Hu*, or West Lake, still one of the most extensive and beautiful gardens in the world. During his historic visit to China on February 21, 1979, President Nixon made a special point of going to Hangzhou to see the West Lake. Here Mao Zedong served Hangzhou's world-renowned *Long guing*, or "Dragon Wells," tea prepared with bottled "Chrysanthemum Water" from the Dragon Wells Source.[5]

Tang impulsiveness gave way to the carefree attitude and cult of youth of the Song. Men studded their dyed hair with flowers in an effort to retain the splendor of youth, and wig-makers reaped fortunes. All flocked to "golden needle houses" for acupuncture facelifts. Defiant of fate, foregoing the spiritual for the temporal, the Song frolicked as if the golden days on earth would never end.

The Imperial Palace—a "pleasure dome" if ever there was one—hummed with courtesans' raucous laughter. Leading the merry masquerade was Emperor Huizong, who was so entirely devoted to self-indulgence and pleasure-seeking that he is frequently called the "Imperial Dreamer." He possessed an astonishing 3,912 concubines,[6] and even if his passion for collecting "new wives" was great it did not preclude an equal fondness for tea. He is remembered as one of the foremost tea lovers in history.

Tea remained the exclusive property of the Emperor, and it was tea that paid for the grandiose imperial life-style. Fortunately for tea historians, Emperor Huizong (ruled 1101–1125), took more than a nominal balance-sheet interest in tea. Inspired no doubt by Lu Yu's *Cha Jing*, or *Classic of Tea*, the Emperor wrote[7] the informative *Ta Kuan Cha Lun* describing in detail Song Dynasty tea.

Descendents of the peasants who had sought refuge in Sichuan province at the turbulent end of the Tang Dynasty formed a large body of experienced Song teamen. They carried their tea knowledge to all parts of China; the large government plantations established by the Tang were restored and great new garden-tea plantations were laid out. Song mandarins goaded by a now-lost imperial decree actively implemented what must have been a national policy encouraging peasants to convert fallow lands into lush garden-tea plantations. In some cases, notably the extreme example of Zhejiang province, highly profitable tea was planted on land traditionally used for the production of food staples. Infant mortality, disease, natural disasters, and war had kept China's birthrate down, stabilizing the population. Thus the Song conversion of food-lands to tea-lands did not result in the multitude of deaths from starvation this same policy caused at the end of the eighteenth century when China's population explosion began.

The vast channelling of economic and human resources into the creation of new tea plantations left little energy to devote to developing new methods of tea production. It is important to note that the "generation" of the millions of tea plants needed for the great Song tea plantations was carried out by raising sprouts from tea seeds, then bunch planting them with intercropping of hemp or millet. This was the ancient seeding method perfected during the Tang Dynasty.

Song Dynasty tea presents many curious paradoxes, among them the fact that although garden-tea plantations were laid out on a vast scale it was an exaggerated desire for rare mountain teas that best characterized the Song. They interpreted literally the ancient adage "Fine tea comes from high mountains." Any misty mountaintop permitting the growth of even a single tea bush became a possible site for cultivating a coveted Song tea. Many serious, profit-oriented teamen, unlike the tea-crazy hermits of the Tang Dynasty, cultivated tiny tea plantations on practically inaccessible mountain cliffs. Pickers risked life and limb to harvest a few precious tea leaves each year, but the danger was worth braving for teas valued at more than their weight in gold. These mountain "cliff teas" were so rare they became legendary even during their own time. Needless to say, cliff teas were the great exception to the rule and only a select happy few within the imperial entourage actually got to taste them. Less dangerous to harvest yet still quite lucrative was tea planted on well-drained eastern slopes of high mountains subject to early morning sunshine and afternoon shade, ideal conditions for tea. This mountain "flank tea" was planted on a smaller scale than that of garden-tea. It was the tea from the plantations along mountain flanks that was known to, and coveted by, the nobility and wealthy upper classes of the Song Dynasty.

Tea harvesting continued to be done by hand, work reserved for unmarried girls and young women. Only the exceptionally fine, rare teas grown expressly for the Emperor's personal use were delicately clipped off with gold scissors, the "Imperial Cut" that disappeared with Imperial China. The best teas were transported by relays of rapid horses to insure they arrived perfectly fresh.[8]

The origin of the Imperial Tribute Teas earmarked for the Emperor constituted one of the principal novelties of the Song Dynasty. Whereas the best Tang tea had come from Yang Xian in Zhejiang province, the forty-one Song Tribute Teas including the legendary "Silver Leaves of Ten Thousand Springs Tea" and a tea called "Best Quality Picked Tea" came from Fujian province, the highest rated Song tea growing region. Foremost among the Fujian plantations was the Emperor's "forbidden" Pai Yuan Garden on Wu-I (Bohea) Mountain, which produced the powdered white tea preferred above all others by Huizong. In Fujian, as elsewhere across China, the smallest leaves, the tender pekoe, were all reserved as Tribute Tea for the Emperor.[9]

Fresh tea leaves were graded prior to processing into five categories based on the size of the leaves, a criterion used to judge the quality of tea leaves since at least the Three Kingdoms Period. (Today, however, tea is graded *after* processing in a complete reversal of ancient methods; modern loose tea had not been invented by the Song Dynasty and traditional tea manufacture still prevailed.) As before, all fresh tea leaves were steamed and then molded into cakes. Song cake tea had a characteristic triangular shape and a light purple color due to the addition of plum juice, which was required to combine the solid cake of tea. Most cakes weighed one *jin*, or slightly over one pound. Brick tea destined for export principally to Tibet continued to be produced, while a new solid ball-shaped tea was introduced for the domestic market. Obviously, the quality of Song tea leaves had to be determined *before* they were compacted into cakes of tea, whereas modern loose leaf tea is always graded after processing.

Tea merchants had no other way of reconciling the paradox of a high demand for hill-tea and their great stocks of garden-tea than by lending the latter a flowery name. Chinese tea buyers were astute (or at least wary, which is half the way to wisdom) and not easily hoodwinked by false claims. In order to be passed off for something they were not, the teas were given names such as "Misty Mountain Tea," "Garden in the Sky Tea," "Cloudy Mountain Tea," "Sparrow's Tongue Tea," or "Falcon's Talon Tea."[10] This example of ancient marketing might be construed as misleading, but it was not fraudulent. In the absence of a better tea classification system the use of flowery tea names proliferated during the Song dynasty, a regrettable trend. Unfortunately, these often-elaborate, early brand names were largely employed to disguise inferior teas, which prompted Emperor Huizong to lament the wholesale tea trafficking and frauds perpetrated during his reign.

As we have seen, solid, triangular-shaped, purple-colored cakes of tea each weighing about 1.3 pounds comprised the usual form of Song Dynasty tea. Adherence to the ancient cake tea tradition was even reaffirmed when compacted ball-shaped tea was introduced. Yet, it is a striking paradox that the rarest, costliest, and most coveted Song tea was not solid at all, rather a powdered tea so fine that the slightest breeze could set it wafting away.

Among the many innovations devised by the ingenious, talented Song, powdered tea (*mo cha* and *nian cha*)[11] distinguished their dynasty from all others. The name of the man who developed Song powdered tea is lost to history, but chances highly favor a Buddhist monk or a tea-crazy poet living as a hermit. Perhaps a Tea Master invented powdered tea, because Tea Masters became practically indispensable for preparing it and they no doubt saw this as the guarantee of a sinecure. Only a few initiated monks and trusted teamen in the "forbidden" imperial tea gardens, however, knew the secret of making it, since tea leaves destined to become powdered tea underwent a processing unlike any other tea variety.

Once the young shoots, or pekoe, of special cliff-hanging tea bushes had been picked they were immediately put into a sack that was sealed inside an airtight earthenware jar. Months later the jar was opened and the desiccated tea leaves were pulverized to form a fine powder. Sieves of increasingly finer netting were employed to insure uniformity.[12]

Powdered tea alone proved to be an exciting tea adventure, heightened still further by its various colors ranging from shades of green to an astounding white. Indeed, white tea was the great novelty of the Song Dynasty. Of the twenty teas described by Emperor Huizong, he declared it to be his favorite.

Tea plants are evergreens whose leaves do not change color as the seasons change; no extraordinary tea plants grow white leaves (or black or any color except green). It is the processing that fresh green tea leaves undergo after harvesting that determines their final color and aspect. Although the tea leaves used in making white tea resembled those used to make other tea varieties, only leaves from wild tea bushes growing on isolated cliffs were deemed worthy enough to be used to make white tea. "Priceless" white tea's costliness was, therefore, due to the rarity of these wild tea trees and the patient steps and care taken in its manufacture. Today China exports a "white tea" called Pai Mu Tan produced in Fujian province, but this tea is actually an Oolong and bears no resemblance other than name to Song Dynasty white tea.

The rarest powdered teas were destined for the tea dishes of the Emperor and his entourage, while all others had to make their own powdered tea from cake tea. An extremely sharp knife was used to cut small pieces from a solid cake of tea; these were ground to a fine powder that was carefully sifted several times to remove any lumps. Several special utensils were required to prepare powdered Song tea, among them knives, grinders, sieves, and whisks, and this teaware was beautifully crafted.

While water was brought to boiling a small amount of tea powder was placed in a *qián*, a unique saucer-shaped dish devised by the Song to both infuse and drink tea. Special dark brown and black glazed *qián* were produced because they highlighted the color of white tea, but exquisite white and green glazed Longyuan ceramic *qián* were more customary. Longyuan ware was highly valued for its attractiveness but it became an important export article, mainly because it was thought to reveal the presence of poison.[13]

Boiling water was poured onto the powdered tea and the mixture was beaten or "whipped" with a whisk, producing a frothy foam. Beating had the added advantage of replacing the oxygen lost while boiling the water. Emperor Huizong's white tea would be a pure white, while teas of lesser quality bore an undesirable gray or yellowish cast. Green tea gave a cherished green foam called "Jade Froth."[14]

By the time the tea had cooled sufficiently to permit drinking the suspended tea particles had settled at the bottom of the *qián*. If one was careful not to roil the liquid one could sip the tea over the rim of the *qián* without having to filter it.

Once again, boiling water was poured onto the sludge-like tea residue and it was vigorously whipped, allowed to cool, and then drunk, a procedure repeated as many as seven times. This indicates that the Tang poet Lu Tung's proverbial "Seven China Cups of Tea" had been taken literally by the Song, who were ever anxious to revive ancient traditions. Contrary to expectations, however, the seventh *qián* of tea would not have been bitingly bitter. This is because powdered tea precipitated out of solution rapidly, having infused only slightly each time.

Salt, cloves, the onion-like *pesai*, and other sweet spices used to flavor Tang tea were banished from Song tea tables, although some aromatic substances were still used to scent tea. Imperial teas had been scented during the Tang Dynasty and the custom was continued by the Song, as described by Cai Xiang: "Although tea has a natural fragrance the Emperor's tea has its fragrance enhanced by mixing in a minute amount of borneol and other extracts."[15]

Unfortunately, Cai Xiang did not list the "other extracts" used to scent Imperial Tea, but likely possibilities are essence of tea and jasmine flowers or essence of long-life lotus and chrysanthemum flowers. Here it is important to realize that the scenting was done with the essential oils of the flowers used to make cake tea, not with the flower petals (they would be used to scent tea only in the Ming Dynasty).

Another singular paradox regarding Song tea is that although they produced a proportionally greater amount of tea than other dynasties (relative to China's overall population), it was disproportionately costlier than tea in other periods. A valuable tea inventory and price list written by Emperor Huizong informs us that a cake of the best tea was simply "priceless." In order of descending quality the other grades cost fifty-seven grains of gold, twenty-eight grains of gold, and fourteen grains of gold[16]— truly imperial prices for an Emperor living in a palace of "coral forests and jade halls." A commoner could live for four to five months on five ounces of silver or set up a tea-shop with fifteen ounces of silver.[17] The high price of tea had the undesirable effect of inciting unscrupulous tea falsification, which became a plague of the Song Dynasty.

The exorbitant price of quality tea certainly excluded the vast majority of Chinese tea drinkers, who had to content themselves with large-leaf "After the Rains Tea." The prosperous upper class, on the other hand, demanded good tea and were willing to pay the inflated prices that authentic and rare teas commanded.

It would be false to believe that whipped tea enjoyed any but limited favor during the Song Dynasty. A bond similar to the one linking the French nobility to the Catholic clergy in seventeenth-century France bound the nobles of the twelfth-century Song Dynasty to Buddhist monks. These formed the restricted group of whipped tea drinkers.

During the Tang Dynasty Po Zhang had written a guide for monastic tea usage. This described the monks' tea harvesting before a statue of Buddha and the ritual performed by special monks called *Cha Tu*, or "Tea Keepers," charged with offering sacrificial tea to Buddha. Monasteries in Song times had developed a rigid hierarchy in which middle-ranking priests called "Masters" took care of the sutras, halls, rooms, alms and bath houses; after them came the "Keepers" of the kitchen, vegetable garden, and tea. Tea Keepers prepared the large bowl of tea from which the brothers communally drank. With the advent of whipped tea the monks' collective tea drinking evolved into a ritualistic tea ceremony. Ironically, as the tea ceremony began to wane in China it found a new home in Japan. Song-style whipped tea remains the basis of the Japanese tea ceremony, or *chanoyu*, which is not an occasion for entertaining and is best suited for Zen monks and hermits. It is indeed unfortunate that the Japanese did not adopt the convivial, urbane attitude of the Song along with Song-style tea. On the subject of tea and friendship, Lin Yu Tang advised:

The proper enjoyment of tea can only be developed in an atmosphere of leisure, friendship and sociability, for it is only in the company of those gifted with a sense of comradeship, extremely select in the matter of forming friends and endowed with a natural love of the leisurely life that the full enjoyment of tea became possible. Take away the element of sociability and these things have no meaning.[18]

Tea is a bridge between people and as such it has often been called the oil of Chinese civilization. Indeed, the "sociability" associated with tea is China's greatest legacy to the world.

Offering a cup of welcoming tea to a guest dates back to Laozi's follower, Guangyin. By the Tang Dynasty hosts had begun serving "Greeting Tea" to every visitor, a custom already widespread during the Song Dynasty when Chinese tea manners were formalized.

Social rules governing tea manners were invariable (and inviolable), but Song tea etiquette certainly did not regulate a religious tea ceremony. Burning incense and offering rice and tea at the family altar—duties performed by servants—fulfilled all religious obligations and were the extent of the tea ritual.

Song homes were anything but halls of meditative silence. Whenever friends came for tea it was a joyous, noisy occasion with animated conversation, gossip, jokes, and laughter. Except for the Edwardian Britons, no other group has been as tea-party loving as the Song. If a parallel is sought, both were enjoying the fruits of a prosperous empire with immense wealth for leisure and gracious living. Parlor games were much in style during the Song Dynasty and teatime was the perfect occasion for playing them. One of the most popular, yet expensive, games of the upper classes was *Ta Cha*, or "Tea Contest." Although invented by the Tang the game was revived by the Song, who played it with a passion. To play *Ta Cha* a judge was first designated, then each contestant in turn prepared an unnamed tea of his choice with pure water brought from special springs. The object of the game was for each player to guess where the different teas had been grown, and winners received costly prizes offered by the host.[19] The discovery of an unknown tea or tea-water source was a guarantee of social success in addition to an excellent occasion for displaying one's wealth. With the numerous tea plantations worldwide today, *Ta Cha* would be an exciting game to play even now.

Song tea customs were generalized throughout China. Thus it is possible to follow along in the steps of a visitor invited for tea in a Song mansion and thereby observe the tea manners practised in thousands of Song households.

The visitor passed through a moongate into the mansion compound and slowly strolled along a stone walk, taking time to appreciate the "Ten Views" of a landscaped formal garden. He might stop momentarily in any of several ornamental pagodas or pavillions, or from a zig-zag, gaily painted bridge he might peer into a water-garden, marvel at the beauty of the aquatic plants, and admire the bulbous-eyed, multicolored fish whose fins resembled angel wings.

After he arrived in the mansion's south-facing entrance hall, numerous servants busily removed the guest's fur-trimmed outer garments and straightened his long-gown, a floor-length, exquisitely embroidered "tea-gown" fastened down the side, with long, large-cuffed sleeves covering his hands. He was then escorted at a leisurely pace to one of the "honor halls," either the western or southern drawing room, barely revealing white socks and silk shoes under the hem of his tea-gown as he walked.

A polite host informed by servants of the visitor's arrival stood waiting in the honor hall to welcome the guest. Allowing an expected guest to wait was an insulting breach of etiquette, but anyone arriving unexpectedly could be put off by servants saying, "Master is not free today, please come another time and he'll invite you to tea."[20]

The host and guest bowed to each other (never shaking hands) before the ever-present tea table symbolizing Chinese hospitality. Song tea tables were not low like modern coffee tables, but were raised like dining tables. Rectangular in shape and large enough to seat four to six people comfortably, Song tea tables ranged in style and costliness from the intricately carved, elaborately decorated lacquer tea tables of the rich to the common bamboo tea tables of modest homes.

After bowing in greeting the host and guest seated themselves on opposite sides of the tea table. In North China during the cold winter months, however, the tea table served a merely symbolic role because there people lounged upon the cushioned, heated *kang*.

Etiquette required every host to offer tea, usually served automatically as soon as everyone had been seated, but a guest could refuse it whereupon wine was served instead.[21]

The Song were among the most knowledgeable tea drinkers in history. Since they spent enormous sums buying quality teas, they did not risk wasting any by preparing it badly. Wealthy families employed a fulltime Tea Master who was responsible for buying choice teas, procuring pure tea-water, and preparing tea for the family and guests. Having a Tea Master on the household staff carried considerable prestige. Many merchant-class families who could not afford a fulltime Tea Master hired an itinerant Tea Master (these always seemed to be ex-monks) whenever they hosted a tea party or aped their betters and played *Ta Cha*. No matter who made the tea and regardless of the condition of the host serving it, all guests were made to feel honored and teacups were always placed before each person respectfully with two hands.

Practicality rather than etiquette dictated that teacups never be more than four-fifths full. Song teacups had no handles, and once boiling tea had been poured into them the sides became scorching hot and could not be touched. However, if the teacups were only four-fifths full the rim remained cool and could be held with the index finger and the thumb in a crab-grasp, allowing one to drink hot tea without burning either the lips or fingers. The vice-like crab-grasp also permitted a tighter, more controlled hold of the teacup, thus minimizing the risk of spilling any tea. To spill tea was doubly unfortunate, for in addition to the discomfort of having burning tea fall into one's lap, spilling tea was high on the list of Song society's *faux pas*.[22]

The dexterous Chinese who ate with chopsticks had no problem mastering the crab-grasp hold of a teacup, but the difficulty was many times increased for the great mandarins wearing finger-guards. Women's feet were bound to show they did no work and in the same spirit men allowed their fingernails to grow. Often these reached as many as six inches in length. Such long nails were extremely brittle, so scabbard-like finger-guards made of gold or silver encrusted with precious jewels were worn to protect them. As the hands were moved the finger-guards touched each other, making a continuous clicking sound.

Salted nuts and seeds, sweetmeats, or fruit were often served with tea but no host was under the obligation to serve any food.

Prior to a guest's departure a final, purely symbolic cup of tea was always served. This display of good manners meant that the guest's company was so pleasurable it was a shame he could not stay longer. However, a polite guest knew his cue and did not drink any of this tea. Rising to his feet, as he took leave of his host it was customary for the guest to say, "Thank you for the tea," even if he had drunk no tea at all.

THE TEAHOUSE

The Tang invented the Tea Master, the Song the teahouse. After the tremendous success met by the first teahouses, they quickly mushroomed to rival taverns in number. Before the end of the Song Dynasty teahouses had spread throughout the Empire and could be found in small remote villages and some quite unexpected places. Truly omnipresent, teahouses came to occupy such an important place in Chinese daily life that one wonders how they had previously gotten along without them.

One entered any teahouse and chose a vacant seat at any tea table. In multistoried teahouses a cup of tea cost proportionately more as one went higher up.[23] Almost as soon as one was seated a teahouse waiter (teahouse waiters seemed to materialize magically from thin air) asked the customary question, "What kind of tea would you like, Sir?"

It was possible to order steeped tea or spicy, sugared ginger tea or any of several varieties of name-teas. Other beverages such as sour plum drinks, spring water, and warm wine were available as well. On each table sat a bowl of salted pine nuts, walnuts, or melon seeds, offered free of charge because eating them caused a thirst that would be quenched with a paid drink.[24]

Every teahouse prepared snacks and light meals, often providing res-taurant and catering service as well. The fare varied depending on the culinary talents of each teahouse cook but generally teahouse food was excellent, the most delicate and tasty food in all China. A hundred different dishes, including piping bowls of noodles, meat, and fish dishes, hot steamed buns, date pudding, and an infinite assortment of imaginative pastries might be found on the copious menu.[25]

People began and ended their day in the teahouse, which acted as both a business and social center. Traders used the teahouse as an office, receiving clients at the tea table and conducting all their business over steaming cups of tea. Soothsayers and marriage brokers were permanent fixtures in large teahouses, where the only trades not plied seemed to be dentistry and tatooing. Even criminals met in the teahouses, and a most lucrative arrangement for any teahouse owner was renting out a private room in the back for the illicit dealings of very shady men. These "eyeless and earless rooms" brought a teahouse owner a "bounty" of taels of silver if he warned the criminals of the arrival of the police in time to escape.[26]

Teahouse owners frequently showed as much business acumen as tea knowledge. It was well known that teahouses always had plenty of cash on hand; many acted as unofficial banks to guarantee gamblers' wagers or accord loans at usurious interest rates for marriage dowries, buying a house, setting up a shop, or funding business deals such as trading in tea, precious metals, or real estate. Several teahouse owners made enough money to prepare sons for the Civil Service Exams and many a great mandarin counted among his ancestors a hard-working teahouse owner.

Teahouses were best known, however, as places where one could relax and have a good time. Friends met in a favorite teahouse to while away the hours chatting or playing dice, dominoes, majong, Chinese checkers (played on a six-branch, star-shaped board), and chess.

Upon leaving the teahouse familiar patrons customarily said, "Charge the tea," no matter what they had eaten or drunk. Businessmen full of their own self-importance might call out, "Charge his tea to me!" pompously paying for another's food and drink to show that his business was prosper-ous.[27]

As a general rule teahouses extended credit (it was widely assumed teahouse owners were well enough connected with the criminal under-ground to hire strongarm collectors) but the decision to do so was at the discretion of each teahouse owner, who judged customers literally at face value. The only case when a total stranger was given unlimited credit was after a regular customer had vouched for him; in this case to refuse credit was an insult to the regular customer.

Promontories in the beautifully landscaped, impeccably maintained city parks were dotted with hexagonal-shaped teahouses with graceful curved eaves that were indistinguishable from pagodas. Of course, the function of these teahouses was not religious because they were intended to be "relaxing spots" from which to contemplate the view and enjoy tea and a beautiful day. These were history's first tea gardens. Today several Song Dynasty teahouses around Hangzhou's famous West Lake have been restored to their former glory and are once again open to the public, who flock to them on pleasant sunny days for family outings to drink tea. Only the clothing styles remind us that the Song Dynasty ended seven centuries ago.

TEAHOUSE ENTERTAINMENT

Few people would think of teahouses as entertainment and cultural centers, yet during the Song Dynasty this was one of the teahouses' important roles, especially in smaller communities.

Whereas the Tang had gloried in the flowery classical language of poetry that pushed the Chinese language to its lyrical limits, the Song preferred picaresque *Hua ben*, or "vernacular tales," in the earthy street language. A whole body of slangy, realistic literature developed especially for the teahouse in the form of spoken novelettes, either *xiaoshuo* (short stories) or *jiangshi* (long epics), which were forerunners of Ming Dynasty novels.[28] These edifying *romans de vérité* became stock entertainment— and enlightenment—in the teahouses. Every large teahouse hired talented story-tellers to draw a crowd and many teahouse story-tellers enjoyed the same popularity as their troubadour counterparts of Medieval Europe. Teahouse story-tellers' bard-like memory was nothing short of prodigious, and it was said at the time that an average of over three hundred stories formed the repertoire of most story-tellers. As always, talent determined success and good story-tellers were accomplished actors able to change their voices across a wide scale of tone and color while adapting their facial expressions to countless quickly changing moods. Though none became rich, teahouse story-tellers earned a good living and a few became famous. Wang Yuan Chi is one teahouse story-teller remembered throughout the centuries for having said, "The delicate bitterness of tea is like good advice."[29]

Many teahouse story-tellers struck out on their own, joining the multitude of street performers. All a story-teller had to do to set himself up in business was buy some tea, a tea kettle, a small stove, a few pieces of charcoal, and several cups and hire a spot on a busy street where there was enough room for people to crowd around. "Come one and all and hear an unbelievable tale for the price of a cup of tea!" hawked the story-teller to draw a crowd. As people gathered about him he served tea and spun his yarns; the story was free but one paid for the tea.

Any subject that played on the heartstrings, tickled the funny bone, or captured the imagination provided a worthy plot for a teahouse story, and many tales heard in modern China derived from stories told in Song teahouses. It is well worth quoting in its entirety the short story entitled *The Miser* translated by Lin Yu Tang, because this story contains an exemplary allusion to tea and perfectly illustrates the type of story told in Song teahouses:

There was a certain miser who, hearing about the reputation of a greater miser than himself, went to the other miser's home to become his apprentice. As usual he had to bring some present to his new master and brought with him a bowl of water with a piece of paper cut in the form of a fish. The great miser happened to be away from home and his wife received him. "Here is my fish as a humble present from your new pupil," remarked the visitor. The miser's wife received it with thanks and brought up an empty cup and asked him to have tea. After the pupil had pretended to drink tea the miser's wife asked him to help himself to some tea-cakes by drawing two circles in the air with her hand. At that moment in came the master miser who, seeing his wife draw two circles, shouted angrily at her, "What extravagance! You are giving two tea-cakes! A semicircle would do!"

Because Song literature was written in the street vernacular that best expressed the universality of human sentiment, Song short stories, epics, and dramas seem strikingly modern. Men today can laugh, cry, love, hate, and feel anger and injustice just as the Song did.

Theater was another fashionable Song passion. Plays were performed in teahouses, thus giving rise to a special variety of drama tailored expressly for the teahouse. Called *zhugongdiao*, or "teahouse drama," these consisted of dramatic sung or recited ballads akin to Song *zaju*, or "Wenzhou drama," developed in Zhejiang province.[30] This "Shanghai drama" as it came to be known strongly resembles German *Singspiel* (one naturally thinks of Schubert, which helps to explain why it was so popular with the Song).

Tragedy, comedy, and scenes of daily life were popular teahouse drama themes; the nagging wife, bribed policeman, immoral monk, shifty crook, tax collector, miser, and scholar were among the favorite stock characters. Teahouse dramas were always in two acts because during the first act the noisy audience hardly paid any attention to the actors but they calmed down to listen to the second act, which all knew to be the best part of the play.

Any teahouse could be modified into a theater by setting a stage at one end of the room. There was no curtain, and except for a balcony, a few tables, and chairs there were neither scenery nor props because dialog alone was relied upon to paint the scene. Costuming was kept to a strict minimum; for authenticity most actors wore their own street clothes on stage.

Teahouse actors, as well as story tellers, were free-lance professionals working a circuit. They stayed for a while in one teahouse before moving on to another in another city, thereby preventing any staleness. An average actor's repertoire numbered more than one hundred different roles although most played character parts, ad-libbing the dialog rather than reciting it from memory.[31]

An immensely popular form of entertainment for over eight hundred years, teahouse drama almost disappeared with teahouses during World War II. However, teahouse drama survived and is once again showing signs of making a strong comeback.[32]

Teahouses flourished everywhere, even in the "breeze and moonlight" quarters (red light districts) of large cities. Nestled among scores of "blue houses," or bordellos, were the "breezy teahouses" that were not houses of assignation (a common Western misconception) but rather semi-private clubs where accomplished courtesans resided. These teahouse courtesans were versed in poetry, singing, and dancing, and they provided cerebral rather than physical entertainment. This distinguished them from "wild flowers" (prostitutes).

A well-advised patron entered a breezy teahouse and, once seated, was asked for his preference in tea. Unlike ordinary teahouses, when the tea was served the patron had to pay on the spot for the *tien hoa ch'a*,[33] or "choice of flowers cup of tea." Reassured that she had seen the client's money, the hostess led him upstairs to rooms where he was served wine, paying immediately the *che kieo*,[34] or "drink money." Following this the breezy teahouse's resident courtesans were presented to him.[35]

In all teahouses and at all times trouble over tea was considered a serious matter. Its gravity is revealed in the proverb, "Murder can be forgiven but insult over tea, never." Human nature being what it is, one can expect voices raised in anger and occasional affrays to be part of teahouse life, although there were probably no more altercations in Song teahouses than in modern cafés. Overwhelmingly, teahouse customers were satisfied with the drinks, food, service, and entertainment they found there, but disgruntled Song teahouse patrons were actually known to threaten, "Don't make me mad or I'll smash up your place and turn it ass over tea kettle!"[36] At the opposite end of the passion scale the Chinese politely exclaimed at an unexpected joy, "It's as welcome as a teahouse fire!"[37] This alludes to the fire always burning for tea water in every teahouse that was such a welcome sight on cold days.

The preceding expressions show that a civilization is mirrored by its language. Omnipresent tea was naturally reflected in the speech of the Song. For example, although Hangzhou's residents were notorious drinkers of amber *kao liang* and red rose wine, everyone had a cup of sobering tea within reach. Whereas Tibetans measured distance in terms of tea where "one tea" equalled 1.65 miles,[38] the Chinese employed it for measuring time. "It happened in less time than it takes to drink a cup of tea" became the usual way of saying "quickly." A man inquiring after a friend in a teahouse might be told, "He's been gone the time it takes to drink a cup of tea,"[39] in other words, "He's just left." "As big as a tea kettle" and "the size of a teacup" became standard Chinese volume measures in the same way that cup and spoon measures were used by Europeans and American cooks.

The word "tea" itself was widely used as an adjective of color, just as "snuff-colored" was used by the eighteenth-century English. The Chinese highly valued "tea-colored silk" and admired finely crafted "tea-colored Chengdu fans." "Tea-colored" meant "green" of course, a description as universally understood in ancient China as the expression "salmon-colored" is today.[40]

A perfect illustration of both tea's influence on the Chinese language and its reputation among the Song is the poignant comparison of "good deeds" to "handing out tea on a hot day." Friends even greeted themselves with "Have you already had tea?" instead of "Good morning."[41]

Song tea manners required serving tea as a courtesy at particular times, for which each tea bore a name. Unlike the flowery, poetic names given tea varieties, names of the teas of courtesy were surprisingly straightforward. The first welcoming cup of tea served to a guest was called "Greeting Tea." With descriptive simplicity offerings of tea to Buddha were named "Sacrificial Tea." New neighbors were always sent a welcoming gift of tea and tidbits called the "Pleasure at New Neighbors Tea." A curious exception to the rule is the cup of tea often depicted in erotic drawings that bore no specific name. Perhaps this was done intentionally, thereby leaving the name up to the imagination.[42]

Teahouses, the manner of preparing tea, and tea customs assumed individual characteristics across Song China. No other group of people can match Song tea diversity; no other group has equalled the Song's inquisitiveness with regard to tea, a restless, often futile quest for new varieties and ways to prepare it. Great innovators, the Song are remembered principally as the originators of the tea ceremony and whipped tea, but without a doubt their greatest achievement was the development of loose tea.

LOOSE TEA

Foreign trade played an important role in the Song Dynasty. Important quantities of goods were carried between East and West along the Silk Road, while great ocean-going ships 100 feet long accommodating 1,000 people and 100 tons of freight plied the Asian waters. These ships used for the first time the important Chinese invention called the "magnetic needle," or compass. Later, China's sea commerce would play a great role, but during the Song Dynasty the overland trade with her near neighbors was vastly enriching for China. This inter-Asian overland trade proved crucial in determining a major turning point in the history of tea.

On China's southern border the Song and the Xia (Tibetans) concluded a treaty requiring an annual Song gift of 72,000 taels of silver, 153,000 bolts of silk, and 30,000 *jin* of tea in return for Tibetan assurances of peace.[43] Trade was encouraged along the Song Empire's northern border as well; silk, rice, porcelain, and tea were exchanged for camels, hides, sheep, wool, and horses. Since ancient times the Chinese had highly valued the swift, well-built horses raised by the "barbarians" living outside the Great Wall. Men of the Tang Dynasty had paid fortunes to own one of the prestigious Ferghana breed immortalized in the unsurpassed beauty of Tang five-color glaze statues. "Barbarians," however, were not interested in the bills of exchange invented by the Tang or in the paper money (*jiaozi*, or "exchange medium") invented by the Song. They accepted as payment only bartered goods. Tea bricks used in trading with Tibet had been one of the first international monies and tea was among the goods used to pay for foreign horses. The ancestors of the Turks, the Tabghaçs of Central Asia, procured tea in exchange for their horses[44] as did the Mongols and the Manchus. This trade became so important that a government agency, the powerful Horse and Tea Commission, was established specifically to regulate it. A monopoly of the Emperor and a mighty generator of his wealth, the Horse and Tea Commission flourished for centuries, developing new tea varieties to satisfy China's "barbarian" clients.[45]

Literary sources from the Song Dynasty remain surprisingly silent about Sichuan's teas although Sichuan was China's biggest tea producer. No longer did poets sing its praises. This decline in Sichuan's reputation—strictly a Song viewpoint—can be considered a kind of negative proof that its teas had undergone a change not to the Chinese liking, allowing the inference that Sichuan, the birthplace of tea, is probably the birthplace of loose tea as well. Sichuan produced vast quantities of tea for export, thereby greatly enriching her tea merchants whose control of the tea market was second only to that of the Emperor. Furthermore, as intermediaries between the "barbarian" and domestic markets, Sichuan's tea merchants controlled China's international trade.

Green loose tea "having a slight taste of fish" was drunk in the Muslim lands of the Himalayas, a very different kind of tea from the brick-tea drunk in Tibet. Tea traveled along the Silk Road to Kashgar where it was the principal beverage, sold in the market there in "baskets having many kinds of tea leaves, all aromatic and no two smelling alike." Kashgar innkeepers charged guests for the amount of water as well as for the number of tea leaves used to make each cup of tea. Tea was drunk along the Silk Route up to Balkh; here its progression abruptly stopped, replaced by the delicious Arab beverage *qawah*. Tea remained unknown in the rest of the Middle East and Europe.[46]

Loose tea was drunk outside China but was it also drunk within the Celestial Empire? The *Classified Outline of the Four Seasons (Si Shi Lei Yao)*[47] states that the Song tea merchants had begun "to replace the traditional cake and ball-shaped tea by loose tea," although it remains uncertain to what extent.[48]

How fortunate we would be to have a stocklist of teas from one of Hangzhou's open-fronted tea shops. This city was a great emporium through which all the teas of the Empire passed. Its tea merchants were no doubt among the first to sell loose tea as a novelty to the avid players of *Ta Cha* who were always eager to discover a new, exotic tea. What was the taste and aspect of Hangzhou's most reputed tea, the costly Precious Thunder Tea? How many varieties of loose tea were available? Where had they been grown? Was black tea produced?[49]

People were justifiably enthused with the ease of preparing loose tea—that is, everyone except the Tea Masters, whose jobs were threatened by it. Teahouse owners especially appreciated loose tea because its easy preparation saved time and it also increased their profits because the price of a cup of steeped tea depended on how many leaves were used. The increasing number of Song teahouses caused a corresponding rise in the demand for loose tea, if not in fact providing the original economic incentive for inventing it.

Centuries-old traditions die slowly. The Chinese were only gradually weaned from cake and ball-shaped tea because despite the ease of preparing loose tea, all literary mentions remark that its taste left much to be desired. Convenience alone was not enough to outweigh the disadvantages of bad taste. Loose tea was after all an export tea developed for "barbarians" living outside the Celestial Empire. Nonetheless, within a few short decades immediately following the end of the Song Dynasty new production methods greatly improved loose tea's taste, and in the next century it predominated almost to the exclusion of all others.

NOTES

1. Precise dating for the period following the Tang Dynasty would be:

5 Northern Dynasties,
10 Southern Kingdoms   907–960
    Northern Song   960–1126
    Southern Song   1127–1279

2. Christopher Hibbert, *Les empereurs de Chine*, trans. Isabelle Reinharez (Paris: Éditions du Fanal, 1982), 105.

3. At various times Nanjing, Kaifeng, and Hangzhou were Song capitals.

4. Hibbert, *Les empereurs*, 104.

5. The renown of a tea is not necessarily a function of its quality. Some of the world's best teas are known to only a handful, while millions can cite the names of low-grade tea.

6. John Blofeld, *L'art chinois du thé*, trans. Josette Herbert (Paris: Dervy-Livres, 1986), 33. The Dutch ambassador to Japan and eminent Orientalist Van Gulik placed the number at 3,000.

7. Although there is no doubt the *Ta Kuan Cha Lun* was written by Emperor Huizong, he surely based his work on that of the Fujian Tea Master Cai Xiang (1012–1068), author of the scholarly treatise *Cha Lu*, or *On Tea*.

8. Blofeld, *L'art*, 35.

9. Zhang Binglun, *Ancient China's Technology and Science* (Beijing: Chinese Academy of Sciences, 1983), 333.

10. Lu Yu, *The Classic of Tea*, trans. Francis Ross Carpenter (Boston: Little, Brown, 1974), 25.

11. Horst Hammitzsch, *Zen in the Art of the Tea Ceremony* (New York: Avon Books, 1980), 26. Lu Yu had deplored "reducing tea to a jade powder and green dust," but this is not to be confused with Song powdered tea (Lu Yu, *Classic*, 119).

12. Hammitzsch, *Zen*, 26–27.

13. I wish to thank the Belgian chemist Yves Van Havere for verifying the legend and proving it true for the family of alkaloid poisons frequently used in the ancient world.

14. Aleíjos, *T'u-ch'uan, grüne Wonderdroge Tee*, 2d ed. (Vienna: Wilhelm Braumüller, Universitäts-Verlagsbuchhandlung, GmbH., 1987), 38.

15. Zhang Binglun, *Ancient China's*, 333.

16. Blofeld, *L'art*, 35.

17. These figures are given in *The Outlaws of the Marsh*, a novel based upon a true historical event occuring in Liangshan Marsh during the Northern Song Period. Although it was written at the beginning of the Ming Dynasty, I have no reason to doubt that the relative values hold for the Song Dynasty.

18. Lin Yutang, *The Importance of Living* (New York: John Day Company, 1937), 221.

19. Jean Runner, *Le thé* (Paris: Presses Universitaires de France, 1974), 17.

20. Quoted from *The Outlaws of the Marsh*.

21. This custom was observed many times in *The Outlaws of the Marsh*.

22. People drinking tea from the large-rimmed *qián* held it with a crab-grasp on each side of the rim in what was actually a double crab-grasp.

23. Blofeld, *L'art*, 74.

24. These beverages and appetizers are mentioned in *The Outlaws of the Marsh*.

25. These teahouse foods are mentioned in *The Outlaws of the Marsh*.

26. The vast majority of teahouses were honest establishments and those frequented by the underworld were few in number.

27. Quoted from *The Outlaws of the Marsh*.

28. Bai Shouyi, ed., *An Outline History of China* (Beijing: Foreign Languages Press, 1982), 285–286.

29. Eelco Hesse, *Tee* 4th ed. (Munich: Gräfe und Unzer, 1985), 15.

30. Bai Shouyi, *Outline History*, 285.

31. Lu Hsun, *A Brief History of Chinese Fiction*, trans. Yang Hsien-Yi and Gladys Yang (Beijing: Foreign Languages Press, 1982), 117–130.

32. See Chapter 12.

33. Ambassador van Gulik's spelling.

34. Ambassador van Gulik's spelling.

35. Robert H. van Gulik, Sexual Life in Ancient China (Leiden: E. J. Brill, 1974), 212–237.

36. Quoted from *The Outlaws of the Marsh*.

37. Quoted from *The Outlaws of the Marsh*.

38. Aleíjos, *T'u-ch'uan*, 39, says the "Tibetans say three cups of tea equal about 8 km."

39. Quoted from *The Outlaws of the Marsh*.

40. A. Chung Sze told me that his father, Ambassador Prince Sze, ordered a "tea-colored" limousine but when it arrived in Shanghai he was distressed at the sight of its bright, copper "Darjeeling Red" color, the color of the tea drunk by the European car makers and not the gold-green color of China tea His Excellency had had in mind.

41. Quoted from *The Outlaws of the Marsh*.

42. The presence of a cup of tea in ancient erotic drawings surely had a sexual signification now lost. Perhaps (since the Three Kingdoms Period?) tea was drunk to avoid the phenomenon sailors and military men call the "whiskey droop." With this thought in mind the presence of a cup of tea in erotic drawings becomes clear. The French seriously addressed the question of tea and sexuality in the article entitled "Pourquoi le

thé est-il aphrodisiaque et le café anaphrodisiaque?" in the *Chronique Médicale*, No. 1, February 1913.

43. Bai Shouyi, *Outline History*, 278. 1 *jin* = 1.3 lbs.

44. "Although they [the Tabghaçs] had drunk tea while in the Chinese sphere, once they had conquered Anatolia (present-day Turkey) they were cut off from their source of tea and ceased drinking it." I wish to thank Mr. André Clot, author of *Soliman le Magnifique*, for this clarification in his kind letter dated February 23, 1988.

45. See Chapter 9.

46. John E. Vollner, E. J. Keall, and E. Nagai-Berthrong, *Silk Roads, China Ships: An Exhibition of East-West Trade* (Toronto: Royal Ontario Museum, 1983), 26–27, 84–86. See also Chapter 4 of this book.

47. Not to be confused with the *Outline of the Four Seasons* (*Si Shi Zuan Yao*) of the Tang Dynasty.

48. Zhang, *Ancient China's*, 332.

49. The lack of documentary evidence concerning the origin of loose tea in the Song Dynasty is due to the upheaval of the Mongol invasion, which occurred at roughly the same time loose tea was first made.

8

Yuan Dynasty
1280–1368

After the separate Mongol tribes had concluded alliances, their combined strength enabled them to raid the Bactrian camel caravans and to literally carry off the riches of China's international trade. Little by little these raids became full-fledged wars of conquest as terrifying bands of Mongols swarmed violently out of the Asian wastes in the thirteenth century to conquer one of history's largest empires.

Leading the bloody rampage was Genghis Khan (1162–1227), whose fitting name meant "Perfect Warrior." Like their Hun ancestors under Attila, the fierce, disciplined Mongol troops traveled hundreds of miles without stopping, chewing raw meat washed down with rancid mare's milk as they rode. They moved as a single fighting unit, literally swooping down on their prey in lightning surprise attacks that left enemies no time to prepare a defense.[1] These murderous marauding bands of Mongols were known by the fearsome name "horde," a word that is still frightful after 800 years. Cruel and merciless, Mongol troops gave no quarter to either men, women, or children along their bloody path. Patrick Fitzgerald in *Ancient China* called them the "most savage and pitiless race known to history."

The Mongols' European advance stopped at the gates of Vienna and along the German border because Medieval Europe was not—fortunately—a sufficiently appetizing morsel. Instead, the rapacious Mongols turned their attention to the richer, more enticing China of the Song, setting their sights on their great neighbor in whose sphere and shadow they had lived for centuries.

An excessive refinement has far too often been cited to explain the Song Dynasty's decline and fall. Reports of Song soldiers selling their horses to buy perfume overshadow the fact that the Chinese had resisted the sustained Mongol pressure on their empire for over 300 years. The Song spent enormous sums on arms to equip men for the protection of their borders. They even gave the Mongols gifts of tea if they remained peaceful. For centuries the Mongols had been kept at bay and even after the capture and exile of Emperor Huizong, the Southern Song fought on for another fifty years, resisting valiantly the swarming Mongol hordes that no other people on earth had been able to hold back.

History has repeatedly shown that great conquerors like Genghis Khan share the fate of dying before their dreams are fulfilled. It was his grandson, Kublai Khan (1215–1294), who completed the conquest of China, founded the Yuan Dynasty, and enjoyed the fruits of victory. Kublai Khan ruled over a vast empire and with the exception of India all Asia was his, making him the richest and most powerful man in the world.

It was Kublai Khan's China that so amazed the Venetian Marco Polo, who lived there for seventeen years (from 1271 to 1294). He had so gained the Great Khan's trust that he was named to the lucrative post of tax collector of Hangzhou.

Polo would have fared better had he remained in China, for upon his return to Italy he was immediately cast into prison for having spread "dangerous lies." There he dictated a "revelation" of the marvels and curiosities he had seen in Yuan China. We are as impressed as Polo by the Honor Hall of the Winter Palace that served as a banquet hall seating 6,000 people. Polo reported that the Mongols drank condensed milk, then unknown in Europe. He wondered at the "special black stone that burns so well that when these stones are placed in the hearth at night they are still burning in the morning."[2] Lu Yu knew of these "black stones" in the eighth century and had recommended their use over wood for boiling tea-water because the smoke of a wood-burning fire imparted an unpleasant odor to tea. Unknown in Polo's native Italy, they had been used for quite a while by the English, who called the miraculous black stones "coal."

It is surprising that there are enormous omissions in Polo's work. We will never know if his book was censored or if he kept his silence by design, because such things as the Great Wall, gunpowder, printing, and kites were not even mentioned. No wonder Polo could say of his book, "I haven't told half of what I saw."

It is hard to understand why Polo never discussed tea even though he was one of the imperial tax collectors and had to levy taxes on it. His only mention of tea occurs when he tells of the misfortune befalling a finance minister who was thrown out of office in 1285 because he had dared to raise the tax on tea.[3]

Polo was a trader, not a scholar. He had gone to China on business intent on making a profit, not as an ethnographer to observe and document Chinese customs. If we had only his book to rely on our knowledge of Yuan China would be limited. Fortunately, however, Polo was not the only European in Yuan China. Perhaps because Kublai Khan's own mother was a Nestorian Christian he welcomed talented men of all nationalities and religions into his empire. His personal jeweler, for example, was a Frenchman named Boucher. Other Europeans there were Benjamin of Tudela,[4] Zuane of Carpini, and Guillaume of Rubrouck, men like Polo whose names have been preserved because they published accounts of their travels to China. From these first European eyewitness accounts we know about the extent of tea's penetration, the types of tea available, their taste and appearance.

Prior to their conquest the Mongols had lived a rude, semi-nomadic existence within the vast, isolated confines of Mongolia. The geographic proximity of the Mongols to the Chinese made them neighbors but culturally they were moons apart. Comparable as opposite extremes, the crude barbaric Mongols shared none of the Song love of gracious living. On one side of the Great Wall lived a people who recoiled with disgust from all milk products while on the other side lived the greatest milk drinkers in the world.

The Mongols literally lived on milk. Not just any milk would do, however, because all but equine milk was disdained. Even Mongol children washed down their greasy mutton staple with milk wines, either the thin rank-smelling bluish-white *kumis*[5] made by placing mare's milk in leather sacks where it fermented or the more potent *ankhi* that resembled *kumis* but had a better smell and taste. Butter and cheese were also made from mare's milk, as were the dehydrated milk tablets invented by the Mongols called *grut*. These could be dissolved quickly in water to make a thick, nourishing milkshake.[6] Condensed milk was invented by the Mongols for their armies and they were the first to pasteurize milk. The predominance of milk and milk products in the Mongol diet directly affected Mongol tea customs.

Long before their conquest of China the Mongols had drunk tea. Their only wealth—aside from what they stole—was in horses and as early as the Tang Dynasty these were exchanged for Chinese goods and tea. When loose tea appeared in the Song Dynasty to replace solid ball and cake tea, the Mongols were the first people converted to it. Although loose tea's original taste was barely palatable it did not deter the Mongols who drank a kind of tea the Chinese could never have stomached anyway, namely, milk-tea, a solely "barbarian" drink. The practical Mongols boiled mare's milk to pasteurize it, and since wood was scarce in Mongolia they put the tea leaves in at the same time to make a drink that satisfied their fondness for both milk and tea.[7]

When the Russian caravan trade developed later the Mongols gradually took to drinking brick tea. We are fortunate to have a detailed account by a European observer that describes how the Mongols made tea from tea bricks:

> They use a lot of brick tea which is both a beverage and food for them. The Chinese on the other hand sell vast quantities of this tea but never drink any of it. To prepare this tea they put aside all the dried, dirty and rotten leaves as well as the stems, and after mixing this with a sticky substance they put them into square molds and dry them in ovens. To these square blocks of tea the Russians have given the name "Brick Tea." A piece of this tea is put into a special mortar and ground then the powder is put into an iron bottle filled with boiling water which they leave a long time over the fire, adding only salt and milk. Sometimes they put in some flour fried in oil. This tea, or soup, is known by the name of *satouran*. I've drunk both these kinds of brick tea and I've found they taste alright and I believe they are quite nourishing—everything depends upon the experience and cleanliness of the person who makes the beverage. These square tea bricks also serve as a money or medium of exchange in the markets of these people.[8]

The Mongols were also known to melt pieces of mutton fat and goat cheese into tea.[9]

Before the conquest of China tea flavored with almonds had been a favorite with the Mongols, and there were certainly other ways of preparing tea that reflected individual Mongol tastes.

The Mongol conquest was an important moment in Chinese history and in the history of tea. During the course of the Mongol's short reign the loose tea invented by the Song gained greatly in popularity, setting the stage for its almost total predominance during the Ming Dynasty.

The obvious advantage of loose tea was its easy preparation, but this was cancelled out by its major drawback, a bad taste. However, tea's development—and taste—received an important boost during the Yuan Dynasty when teamen discovered the process of *chaoqing*, literally "roasting out of the green." This made it possible to manufacture whole-leaf tea that tasted good.[10] For the first time tea's taste presented its true flavor. *Chaoqing* also greatly improved the shape of the tea leaves and enhanced the color of their infusion. Tea processing itself was simplified, saving both time and labor.

Chaoqing wrought an immediate revolution in the tea market. With an enthusiasm equal to the Americans' welcome of the tea bag the thirteenth century Chinese eagerly embraced the tasty loose tea that was so easily prepared.

The Chinese wiseman Ye Lu Zhou Cai played an active role during the Yuan Dynasty as advisor to both Genghis Khan and Ogdai Khan. In his *Collected Works of the Hermit Zhanran* he had foreseen the short life of Mongol rule: "The Empire was conquered on horseback, but it cannot be governed on horseback" (290).

Only eighty-eight years after its founding the Yuan Dynasty was overthrown in a massive, popular uprising.

NOTES

1. H. Lamb, *Genghis Khan: Emperor of All Men* (New York: Bantam, 1953), was the major reference source for this chapter.

2. A. T'Serstevens, *Le livre de Marco Polo* (Paris: Éditions Albin Michel, 1955), 175.

3. Curt Maronde, *Rund um den Tee* (Frankfurt am Main: Fischer Taschenbuch Verlag Gmbh, 1973), 18.

4. Andrew Boyle, ed., *Everyman's Encyclopaedia*, vol. 2 (London: J. M. Dent, 1909), 256. Benjamin of Tudela's book was called *Itinerary*. He actually went only "to the frontiers of China."

5. Lu Yu, *The Classic of Tea*, trans. Francis Ross Carpenter (Boston: Little-Brown, 1974), 168, note 138.

6. Father Henry Serruys, *The Mongols and Ming China: Customs and History*, vol. 1 (London: Variorum Reprint, 1987), 150.

7. W.J.F. Jenner, *Memories of Loyang* (Oxford: Clarendon Press, 1981), 129.

8. M. G. Timkovski, *Voyage à Pékin en 1820–1831*, vol. 1 (Paris: Librairie Orientale de Dondey-Dupré Père et Fils, 1827), 36.

9. S. Yi, J. Jumeau-Lafond, and M. Walsh, *Le livre de l'amateur du thé* (Paris: Robert Laffont, 1983), 20–21.

In Tibet hot green tea was prepared in shallow wooden bowls and after a few sips of bitter tea cheese-like yak butter was melted into the remaining tea and a barley meal having the consistency of sawdust called *Sampa* was added and mixed with the fingers until the paste detached from the sides of the bowl forming a doughy lump as all the tea was absorbed. Pieces of the dough were pinched off and eaten, made more appetizing by adding sugar, salt, vinegar, or fermented bean sauce.

10. *Chaoqing* 炒青 is a *pinyin* transliteration of the expression "roasting out of the green." It is used throughout Zhang Binglun's book *Ancient China's Science and Technology* (Beijing: Foreign Languages Press, 1980), and I have used it here. The closest English equivalent, torrefaction, is commonly used in reference to coffee.

9

Ming Dynasty
1368–1644

When Kublai Khan founded the Mongol Dynasty he gave it the name "Yuan," meaning "the First," a conceit presumptuous enough to have merited divine sanction, yet Kublai possessed imperial grit and proved a wise and able ruler. Durable post roads built on his order throughout the immense Mongol Empire were so safe it was said, "A young girl with a gold nugget on her head can cross the empire safely." Along these trade routes playing cards, printing, and other Chinese inventions traveled to Europe, as well as precious silk and spices. Tea, however, traveled only as far as Persia and remained unknown in Europe.

The force of Kublai Khan's personality had kept the far-flung Mongol Empire together, but at his death inherent weaknesses appeared and the overextended, corrupt empire began to fall apart. Kublai's famous post and trade routes became dangerous.

The Mongol Empire's disintegration resulted from a plague that has infected the lives of men since ancient times, namely, taxation. Mongol greed and avarice had caused increasing tax rises until Yuan Dynasty taxes were among the highest in history. Even "necessities" such as rice and tea bore multiple taxes that priced them out of the reach of the very people needing them most. Moreover, the Mongols foolishly raised taxes even higher when they should have lowered or abolished them. To make matters worse, Yuan tax collectors (among them Marco Polo, the tax collector for Hangzhou) further compounded the people's plight by exacting Shakespeare's "pound of flesh" by severely flogging those who were unable to pay. Abuses and excesses culminated in a spontaneous, massive, and violent peasant uprising, a tidal wave of human fury that Mongol troops could not suppress despite wholesale massacres.

An ugly former monk and sometimes carpenter and beggar from Anhui province named Zhu Yuanzhang became the rebel leader. A clever man, he marched on the capital Dadu at the head of peasant troops and there forced the last Mongol emperor (who, like the tragic Louis XVI of France, spent his time tinkering with clocks) to abandon the Dragon Throne.

The final orders launching the overthrow of the Yuan Dynasty were hidden in round, white mooncakes confected to celebrate their namesake during the Midautumn Festival. The Ming therefore held mooncakes to be doubly sacred and many teahouses adopted the auspicious name "Mooncake Teahouse." Many of these remained in business through the Qing Dynasty. Each year in the fall teahouses competed to confect the best mooncakes.

In a symbolic move Nanjing on the Yangzi River in the heart of China where Chinese civilization had originated was made the new capital. This move demonstrated the Ming desire to revive Chinese traditions interrupted by the Mongol occupation. Zhu Yuanzhang (1328–1398) took the reign-name Hongwu, meaning "Founding Emperor," and declared, "I intend to rule like the Tang and Song."[1]

Despite airy promises Hongwu proved to be a far more absolute ruler than any of the Song emperors had been. The cabal of common ruffians and bandits that ruled Ming China tarnished the dynasty's reputation, leading Orientalists to prefer the China of the Tang and Song. In fairness, however, it should be noted that the much-decried Ming "decadence" actually constituted the engaging naturalistic currents that pervaded Ming civilization, a flourishing epoch in Chinese history that was important in the history of tea and porcelain.

Preferring wine to tea, Hongwu died before he had accomplished little more than founding the Ming Dynasty and spending vast sums of money on his own pleasures. He was succeeded by Yongle, another commoner and self-made emperor. Once again the capital was moved. It was reestablished in the former Mongol capital Dadu, where Yongle ordered millions of trees planted, artificial lakes and canals dug, and monumental palaces and tombs built. The vast scale of this project is astounding; the breathtaking result was a city of unique architectural beauty and harmony renamed "Pe-king," the "Capital of the North" (present-day Beijing).

Ming emperors are not noted for their wisdom and they often stand as prime examples of how not to run an empire. A perfect illustration of imperial impulsiveness occurred one day as Emperor Yongle practised archery in the palace garden. After his arrow hit the bull's-eye he declared,

"If my shot is straight my thinking is right." That same morning he convened his ministers and laid out an ambitious plan of empire-building. It was a throw of dice and luckily the imperial inspiration proved practicable, even profitable for a time.

Admiral Zheng He, a Muslim eunuch from Yunnan province called the "Three Jewel Eunuch," supervised the construction of an armada of sixty-two ships carrying 37,000 men, the largest sailing ships at the time. Each ship was roughly thirty yards in length and could carry a freight weight of 100 tons.[2] Between 1405 and 1433 these "floating cities" completed extraordinary voyages of discovery. They probably went to Australia, because in 1879 a Ming Dynasty statuette was found in the trunk of a baobab tree near Darwin.[3] Zheng He's navigational map exists, appended to the 240–volume *Wu Bei Zhi* by Mao Yuangyi, although the official reports of these voyages were supposedly destroyed "because Zheng He was a enunch."[4]

Scribes accompanying the expeditions tallied the riches of Vietnam, Java, Sumatra, Malacca, Ceylon, Malabar, and the Arabian and African coasts. During their short-lived Age of Discovery the Chinese even rounded the Cape of Good Hope into the Atlantic and were well on the way to discovering Europe—sixty years *before* the Portuguese Vasco de Gama rounded the Cape in 1497.[5] Tea was among the supplies carried on Zheng He's ships and its presence on these epic voyages seems to preview what was to come.

The purpose of the Ming maritime explorations had been to open new markets. Tropical woods, furs, spices, perfume, gold, and silver poured into China, enriching the greedy Ming and financing the rebuilding of the Great Wall (as tourists see it now) and the reopening of the 1,200-mile Imperial Canal connecting North and South China. A direct trading link by sea was established between China and Europe for the first time during the late Ming Dynasty, and it was Ming-style infused tea that was adopted by European tea drinkers.

Whole-leaf loose tea had appeared as early as the tenth century,[6] but it is generally known as Ming-style tea because during the Ming Dynasty it supplanted all other kinds and became the most popular form of tea consumed in China.

Joining Lu Yu's *Classic of Tea* and Emperor Huizong's *Tea Treatise* on the shelf of tea classics was Gu Yunqing's *Tea Manual* (*Cha Pu*), which continued the centuries-old tradition of writing a book to explain new tea drinking styles. Yunqing's *Tea Manual* expertly details the proper way to cultivate, manufacture, and prepare the whole-leaf loose tea predominating in the Ming Dynasty.

The Ming genius was innovative rather than inventive. Tea cultivation and harvesting in the Ming Dynasty showed no changes as ancient methods continued in use; the primary step in Ming tea's manufacture—*chaoqing*, or "roasting out of the green"—had been invented by the Yuan.[7] Even tea customs and teahouses remained much as they had been during Song times. One has a tendency to ask, "So, what did the Ming contribute to tea's development?"

Chinese history is a great lesson in what they term "change within tradition," meaning that traditions were maintained and only transformed as required to meet new demands. Tea had been evolving for millennia, and at crucial periods technical discoveries, passing fashions, and taste preferences wrought changes. Tea was at first chewed, then people thought it was better drunk. Even as a drink it had once been decocted as a tonic, then later stewed with sweet spices to make a pleasant beverage. Over the centuries tea was steeped, whipped, and infused. Solid cake tea ceded its place to bulk loose tea. Centuries of trial and error selected only the most practical, taste-enhancing aspects of tea production and preparation. A new level reached was an improvement on the past, not a break with it. Future generations may develop a new way of preparing tea, but for the last 500 years Ming-style whole-leaf infused tea has provided the world's tea drinkers with the best cup of tea.

It would be wrong to believe the Ming lacked imagination and incentive. Although tea was produced and prepared in the Ming Dynasty as it had been inherited from the Yuan, important innovations were introduced nonetheless.

Since the fifth century "packaged" cake, ball, and brick tea had been traded throughout Asia. These were so tightly compressed there was little fear of spoilage. Ming-style loose tea, on the other hand, presented a nefarious transportation and storage handicap: Bulk tea is fragile and easily spoiled by high humidity, temperature extremes, strong light, or nearness to pervading odors. Even sealed earthenware jars and air-tight lacquer tea chests were no guarantee of freshness. Because loose, whole-leaf tea traveled so badly, we wonder at the state of preservation of the great varieties of "aromatic teas" sold in baskets in Kashgar that had traveled hundreds of miles on camelback, loaded high on the hump above the dust line but still subjected to weather's worst, the stench of camels, and the smoke of campfires. Caravans took tea as far as Balkh in Persia but no farther.[8] Had this been the limit to which tea could be carried overland without spoiling? Was this the reason no tea had ever reached Europe?

Paradoxically, the Ming Empire comprised a considerable, far-flung tea market yet Ming-style loose tea was ill adapted to long-distance travel.

The opening of European markets during the Wanli Period (1573–1620) when tea reached Europe after months of damp sea travel drove the point home to the Chinese. Ming silver lust could bear no loss in tea revenues from tea arriving at its destination in a ruined or rotten state, thus prompting teamen throughout China to strive to resolve the tea preservation problem. Only two solutions were possible: Either improve the packaging or develop a more resistant tea. A multitude of tea containers in all shapes, sizes, and materials must have been tried, but no container was found that bested the bamboo baskets, earthenware jars, and lacquered wooden chests that had been used for centuries. Furthermore, traditional crafting, materials, and shapes continued to be employed in the making of tea jars and tea chests.

Heavy earthenware jars were used primarily for transporting common varieties of garden-tea in areas near waterways because their weight precluded expensive long-distance overland travel. Unchanged since ancient times, earthenware storage jars were sealed with red wax bearing an embossed identifying chop-mark. The earliest known European request for tea is an order from the Dutch Lords Seventeen to their director-general in Batavia for more "jars" of tea.[9] Shipping costly tea in jars to Europe was the best way to insure it arrived in good condition after months spent in the leaky, musty holds reeking of tar and pitch. However, when the volume of the tea trade to Europe increased dramatically in the second half of the seventeenth century shipping tea in earthenware jars was no longer practical. They were replaced by wooden tea chests.

A prime example of Chinese "change within tradition" can be found in the field of ceramics, where the practical Ming displayed their innovative talents to the fullest and outshone all other dynasties in the excellence of their porcelain. Superb Ming porcelain teaware graced Chinese tea tables and for the first time those of Europe as well, where porcelain would help to create a demand for tea.

Sometime during the sixteenth century an enterprising merchant had the novel idea of selling tea in stout porcelain storage jars covered with a matching lid. This ingenious scheme met with immediate success as people snatched up the beautiful blue-and-white (*mei ping*) and five-color (*wu cai*) porcelain tea jars to display in their homes. In many cases they bought a tea solely for its container. These tea jars now worth a fortune would be a prize in any tea lover's collection, but excellent and reasonably priced copies can be bought today in specialty shops. Other tea jars were made of finely engraved gold and silver.

Tea chests and crates—much lighter than earthenware jars—were reserved for transporting hill-tea. Common varieties of tea were packed into simple bamboo shipping crates lined with either *lijian* (waxed paper), rice paper, bamboo paper, or (near silk-producing areas) mulberry paper. Fine teas destined for wealthy mansions were carefully packed in exquisitely decorated lacquer chests or hand-boxes so well crafted that most of those existing today still open and close with a characteristic "woosh" of air, a sure sign of an airtight fit. For added protection a lining of paper was used. Imperial teas and other fine teas were wrapped in silk.

Chop-marks always identified the contents of the tea chests. Common crates were "branded" with ideogram chops burned into the wood with hot, reverse-impression irons. Of course, branding could have damaged expensive lacquer tea chests so these bore chop-marks embossed in wax seals placed over the joined edges. Traces of this wax can still be seen on the tea chests on display at the Nederlands Openluchtmuseum in Arnhem. Unfortunately, ingenious robbers became expert in substituting bad tea for good and then resealing the chests with counterfeit chop-marks; these lucrative transfers were practised on a large scale. The situation finally degraded to a point where all the fine lacquered tea chests and hand-boxes containing expensive teas were fitted with hidden hinges and locked with heavy, ornamental bronze bolt-locks. Priceless rare teas and imperial teas always had to be transported under armed guard.

Tea chests, crates, and hand-boxes came in a puzzling variety of shapes and sizes. This baffling absence of standardization strikes a European as just another Chinese exercise in futility, although a definite logic had been applied in their conception. In general, the smaller the container the more valuable its contents, a truism as valid today as in Ming China. A unit of weight equal to a little over a pound (a *jin*) served as the base measure, and tea containers were designed to hold a volume equal to fractions or multiples of one *jin*. One would logically expect that a regular series of tea containers was made, but the Chinese hold certain numbers to be auspicious and others to be unlucky (like our own number thirteen). Tea containers holding "auspicious" weights were the only ones made, which accounts for the odd variation in Chinese tea containers. Deeply rooted superstitions also played a role in determining the shape of many tea containers, and the extremely popular octagonal "Chinese lantern" forms were especially favored because they had eight sides like pagoda temples.

Chinese hand-boxes used for storing tea were the forerunners of the tea caddies used to store and mix tea that have been found in European and American homes.

Another solution to the tea preservation problem was to modify the tea itself, making it more resistant to long-distance travel. In this field the Ming demonstrated as much innovative spirit as in ceramics. They developed two well-known kinds of tea, black tea and flower-scented tea.

Due to the importance of these teas in the world today it is indispensable to examine their development closely.

Chaoqing, or "roasting out of the green," permitted the manufacture of fine green loose tea that was fragrant and delicate but traveled badly and was easily spoiled. Ming teamen anxious to safeguard tea profits recognized the necessity of rot-proofing tea before it left the factory. Experiments had shown that if tea was allowed to ferment naturally until the leaves turned a reddish copper color and then the leaves were spot heated, this controlled factory rotting resulted in black tea, which the Chinese call "red tea." It is the processing tea leaves undergo that determines their final color, shape, aroma, and flavor. One of the great tea fallacies holds that green and black teas come from different varieties of tea plants. When the Ming developed black tea this did not mean that new tea trees had been discovered, because *all tea leaves are green on the branch*. Both green and black teas can be made from the leaves of the same tree because it is the processing that determines the tea leaves' final aspect.

Since the dawn of Chinese civilization "jade green" was the color of Chinese tea, and the widely used expression "tea colored" referred to the green-colored tea preferred by the Chinese. Had black tea existed in early epochs the descriptive Chinese language would certainly have christened it with a flowery name. This negative proof is supported by an absence of literary mentions of black tea until the Ming Dynasty. No factual basis permits assuming an ancient origin for black tea. Furthermore, all Chinese sources agree that black tea did not appear *by* the Ming Dynasty but *after* its founding.[10] Although black tea became popular in "barbarian lands," it was never appreciated by the majority of Chinese.

The first clients for "export tea" were the "barbarians" living outside the Great Wall. Bartering tea for horses had begun in the Tang Dynasty and for almost 500 years the monopoly of this trade belonged to the powerful Horse and Tea Commission. In 1406 additional horse markets were established on China's northern frontier in order to revive the tea and horse trade, which had fallen into decay.[11] In its best time Liaotung had over 400,000 horses registered.[12] Balance sheet figures for the tea and horse trade (even accounting for fraud) are staggering. Generally, a good horse "cost" 120 *jin* of tea, while an average horse was worth 50 *jin* of tea. In the peak year 1389 more than 20,000 horses were exchanged for one million *jin* of tea.[13]

The Chinese disdained black tea, considering it only worthy of export, but they could not ignore its burgeoning importance. Vast plantations controlled by the Horse and Tea Commission were laid out in Shaanxi province expressly to provide tea for the horse trade.

Profits went, at least in theory, into the Ming treasury, but malignant graft in the Horse and Tea Commission reached truly scandalous proportions and the government hardly profited at all. Students passing the State Exams intrigued for appointments to a lucrative post in the Horse and Tea Commission, where it was well known that an ambitious official could amass a quick fortune for himself and his relatives through "fragrant grease," or bribes. Corruption and smuggling became so rife that action finally had to be taken, and after the death of Emperor Yongle his successor abolished the Horse and Tea Commission on September 7, 1424.[14] However, the smuggling, doctoring, and faking of teas would remain a worrisome plague throughout the Ming and later Qing Dynasties.

Certainly the greatest Ming contribution to the history of tea was the development of flower-scented teas. Few people in history have equalled the Ming's obsessive, impressionist passion for flowers. Any flowers regardless of variety, shape, or color were prized. This spawned a great vogue for flower scroll paintings, flower embroidery on wall hangings and clothes, and pressed-flower albums containing hundreds of different varieties including the pretty white and pink tea blossoms. Epic poems written on a single blossom displayed the incomparable Ming flower fascination. As one might expect, the Ming flower cult influenced tea's development and for the first time flower-scented teas appeared. Scented teas were not new and had been produced at least as early as the Tang Dynasty, but they were made with prohibitively expensive essential oils and were actually reserved as Imperial Tribute Teas. The clever Ming hit upon the novel idea of scenting tea with the abundant, inexpensive flowers they loved so much, making a scented tea the Chinese middle classes could afford.[15]

Two types of flower-scented tea are mentioned in the *Cha Pu*, namely, Lotus Flower Tea and tea scented with the "sweet blossoms" of mignonette, osmanthus, rose, orchid, orange,[16] gardenia, plum, and jasmine. These flowers were preferred over others because they have a high oil content and are consequently quite fragrant. Noticeably absent from the list are the blossoms of the tea plant itself. If tea plants are allowed to grow they become attractive ornamental garden trees similar to dogwoods and cherry trees. Pink and white tea blossoms are best suited for scenting tea leaves and may have once provided the essential oil used in scenting Imperial Tribute Tea, but in the Ming Dynasty planters pinched off all tea flower buds in order to enhance the development of the tea leaves. Since the use of tea blossoms had proved impractical they were replaced by the inexpensive substitutes of jasmine and tea rose, whose natural fragrance is similar to that of real tea blossoms.[17]

Flowers used to scent tea were plucked when half-opened because at that moment their fragrance was considered at its best. Although the quantities of tea to be scented might vary, each time a ratio of three parts tea to one part flowers was rigorously respected. The measured amounts of tea and flowers were put into a porcelain pot in alternating layers until it was full, then the pot was sealed with broad bamboo leaves and set in a caldron of boiling water. After a thorough steaming the pot was emptied and the contents allowed to cool before it was wrapped in rice paper and baked over a fire until dry.[18]

An illustration of the success flower-scented teas enjoyed was the proverbial story of a Ming princess who was so fond of flower-scented tea that she slept with a sachet of it under her ceramic pillow.[19] Flower-scented teas made with fresh flowers and green tea became a court favorite, and in time black teas were also scented, notably with orange blossoms or rose petals. One black tea was scented with Honan province's well-known Rose Congous.[20]

Good scented teas are a complimentary mixture of fragrance and flavor, which is their distinctive feature. Through a peculiar duality scenting can either enhance or mask tea's taste and—alas—scenting was far too often used to disguise the taste of inferior teas.[21] This may be why the upper classes of the Late Ming and Qing Dynasties disdained scented teas, calling jasmine tea "servant's tea."[22]

Lovely, artfully arranged flowers always graced Ming tea tables and for the first time a great variety of sweets appeared there as well. The sweet-toothed Ming had a fondness for sugary confections that was at least equal to their liking for flowers. This caused a major readjustment in tea table fare from predominantly salty foods to predominantly sweet ones. For the first time finger foods are known to have been dunked into the china cups of tea, setting an example Europeans would follow with special tea biscuits. Sweet pastries and candied fruit put into hot tea sweetened it, yet often this sugaring proved insufficient and many Ming tea drinkers habitually added yellow lump sugar (never milk). Dates were the most popular addition to green tea, at once scenting and sugaring it pleasantly. The presence of a few expensive dates in a guest's china cup was a subtle mark of esteem.

During the Ming Dynasty tea was prepared by infusing whole tea leaves, a method familiar to most Western tea drinkers until the invention of the teabag. Five centuries ago tea leaves were placed in a porcelain teapot no bigger than a large orange (the small size reflects tea's high price), and boiling water[23] was poured into the pot. The tea leaves were allowed to infuse for the time it took to inhale and exhale three times, then the tea was poured through a strainer (usually made of bamboo) into the china cups to warm them. After a moment the cups were emptied back into the teapot, where the leaves were again allowed to infuse for the time it took to inhale and exhale three times. After this the tea leaves had sufficiently infused and the brew was ready to drink. As a rule of thumb the teapot was never refilled more than the customary two times, although in poor houses the leaves were infused with several "waters."

Flower scenting, the addition of sugar, and a short infusion time indicate that the traditional Chinese fondness of a bitter taste in tea (once considered the sign of a good tea) was not appreciated by the Ming.

Easily prepared Ming-style tea became everyman's tea. No longer was the expert hand of a Tea Master required, as hosts prepared tea for guests themselves in a dramatic break with the past. Formerly a host's knowledge of the subtleties of tea drinking carried an unqualified snobbishness. Even today the fine art of drinking tea must be learned, although only a happy few are brought up in a tea tradition. The awkward tea manners of new-rich Ming peasants attempting to disguise their humble antecedents can be easily imagined, as can the spilled tea and scorched fingers that caused a terrible loss of face for many.

Chinese tea etiquette remained essentially as it had been since it was formalized by the Song, at least in spirit if not in practice. Generally, the down-to-earth Ming eased existing tea rules and made them less studied and more natural. Ming tea manners no longer required fixed appointments to pay someone a call. Access to officials or men of importance as read in Ming novels could usually be obtained by simply presenting one's large red visiting card (and perhaps a generous tip, or "tea money") to the gateman. Rarely were callers rebuffed—only if a man were too ill or busy to receive visits, or if he were away. Yet this refusal carried with it the obligation to send the caller an invitation to tea at another more convenient time.

Receiving all callers caused home and office *yamen* to be often over-flowing with petitioners. A steady stream of visitors meant that hosts could no longer be expected to stand waiting to receive each guest. Henceforth no one felt offended if he were shown into a reception room from which the host was absent.

Etiquette still rigorously required that every caller regardless of rank or business be served tea upon his arrival, the traditional sign of Chinese hospitality. Hosts receiving visitors all day quickly tired of the drudgery of preparing endless pots of tea (the closeness to the fire made it a hot task as well). Many people must have regretted not having a Tea Master on the payroll. Midway through the Ming Dynasty the prepare-it-yourself attitude toward tea changed. Infused tea was so simple to prepare and failsafe that servants could be trusted to make it. Therefore, hosts sent tea into the kitchens to be readied by servants and it has remained there ever since.

Considering the importance of tea in the daily life of China, tea servants were important members of every mansion's personnel. Tea boys collected tea-water, supervised its boiling, and readied the hot towels given to guests so they could freshen up and wash their hands; tea maids measured out the tea leaves, served the finger foods, and cared for the teaware. Tea servants were the only ones allowed free access to all quarters of large mansions. Separation of the sexes characterized dynastic China; dinner parties, tea parties, and other social gatherings were segregated along gender lines. Gentlemen hosted men-only parties in the men's quarters, while ladies were literally confined to the women's quarters. This strict separation of the sexes did not, however, apply to "sexless" young servants. Tea boys were the only male servants allowed into the women's quarters and they were often bribed by the master to spy on the women's doings, a system that worked both ways. Clever tea boys earned enough "tea money" through spying to set themselves up in business or "buy a quality wife." Others less ambitious squandered their "tea wages" on "wild flowers" (prostitutes).

Serving tea to each of the great many callers could prove to be ruinously expensive over time, so in actual practice hosts asked visitors if they wanted tea and served it only if the guest desired it. Agitated guests were normally served wine, but if they got tipsy they were served tea.[24]

Visits to important mandarins were events involving families, neighbors, and in some cases even entire villages who followed a petitioner's progress as avidly as if they were following the play in a favorite sporting contest. A caller to a powerful mandarin might brag afterward, "He offered me tea twice as if we had known each other all our lives," meaning the visit had gone well. Normally an interview lasted only "the time it takes to drink a cup of tea," meaning between five and ten minutes, and if the host offered no more tea the caller knew to leave. Here occurred the greatest Ming break with the past, for no longer was the symbolic "farewell cup" of tea offered.[25]

Good friends and important guests felt complimented and honored to receive tea three times, whereas not being offered tea was an unpardonable insult. "He didn't even offer me a cup of tea" spoken with venom and disgust became a common expression showing one's anger at another's ingratitude.[26]

Whether receiving at home or in the work place, a host had the obligation to serve tea and nothing more. Depending on the host's means and degree of intimacy with a visitor he might serve alcohol or finger foods such as salted melon seeds, boiled peanuts, sweet Liangziang chestnuts, dried beancurd, steamed buns, sweet Sichuan tangerines, sugary walnut wafers, and other sweets. The list of tea foods was endless and limited only by the imagination of Chinese cooks. Close friends or relatives coming from far away, however, were always served tea and a full meal upon their arrival.

The curious, ancient custom obliging a host to drink before his guest—originally meant to reassure guests that the tea had not been poisoned—continued until modern times for the practical purpose of insuring that the tea had been properly prepared and was suitable to serve to guests.

Except for a brief period during the Song Dynasty when tea was drunk from shallow saucers called *qián*, tea had traditionally been drunk from small handleless tea bowls, the forerunners of European teacups. During the Ming Dynasty divinely inspired porcelain potters flared the rims of traditional china cups and outfitted them with matching saucers and lids, realizing the perfect tea vessel called a *zhong*. The simple yet ingenious design of the *zhong* allows it to function as both teapot and teacup, a design presenting many practical advantages as well as artistic harmony.

The genius of the *zhong* lay in the practical ease of its use. An individual serving of tea leaves was put into the bowl of the *zhong*, then boiling water was poured into it, filling it four-fifths full. The lid was placed over the liquid, serving the double purpose of keeping the brew warm and also holding back any floating tea leaves as the tea was drunk. The saucer permitted the *zhong* to be held and moved about without burning the fingers, while drops and dribbles of tea were prevented from falling onto clothes or tables. Handling a *zhong* requires some practice but the dexterous Chinese manipulated it expertly, an art like using chop-sticks that became second nature.

Since the tea leaves were not strained out of the *zhong*, people had the additional pleasure of seeing the infused tea leaves. Seeing the tea leaves also guaranteed their authenticity and was one way to combat the widespread tea fraud that plagued the Ming Dynasty. This largely accounts for the *zhong*'s enormous success.[27]

When teahouses adopted the *zhong* its use became general throughout China, and for the past 500 years no better vessel for tea drinking has been devised.

Due to religious conservatism ceremonious tea drinking continued to be practiced in many temples and monasteries, but only there. Pilgrims to Buddhist temples were always served tea upon their arrival by the Tea Keeper monk, who was obliged to give pilgrims as many cups of tea as they wanted or as many as were required to "aid their meditation." Affluent pilgrims were expected to give a generous donation to the monastery, and irritable monks thinking too little had been given did not hesitate to berate them, saying, "You've not even given enough money to pay for the tea you've drunk." Poor people paid what they could but some were forced to do a day's work (usually cleaning the latrines) at the monastery to "pay for their tea."[28]

The Chinese possessed an almost innate distrust of monks and dislike for organized religions, although they maintained at least an outward appearance of devotion by dutifully maintaining household altars. Small china cups on family altars contained a few dried leaves of Sacrificial Tea as an offering. Wealthy families annually sent servants laden with large quantities of tea to give to the monks of their favorite temples and to the Keepers of their ancestors' graves, thus "keeping the divinities in tea." A popular tale related the fate of a wealthy mansion's servant charged with transporting Sacrificial Tea. Stopping along the way to prepare a cup of tea with some of the precious load, he was immediately struck dead by a lightning bolt. Moral fables such as this one circulated as warnings to keep servants from selling the "divinities' tea."

Traditionally, beef-flavored noodle soup was served at the end of Chinese meals. However, if someone had vowed for religious reasons not to eat meat he was served tea instead, joining the rest of the company for dessert and cakes followed by after-dinner cordials.

Tea had always been closely associated with China's religions, and by the Ming Dynasty it had become completely assimilated with superstitious beliefs as well. Like another great tea-drinking people, the Victorian English, the Ming were fascinated by the occult. Renowed mediums made fortunes holding popular séances and, as might be expected, omnipresent tea had a role to play. As magic formulas were burned people gazed in spellbound amazement at a sand-tray where an oracle's brush miraculously scratched fateful ideograms in the sand. Mediums always kept a *zhong* of tea readied for the visiting spirit, presented reverently with both hands while kneeling.[29]

Along the streets and in large teahouses soothsayers plied their trade, interpreting fortunes by reading the tea leaves in a person's *zhong*. They enjoyed a brisk business selling roots of tea bushes that were considered good-luck charms.[30]

Tea continued to bear a superb reputation among Chinese physicians. The *Cha Pu*'s author had none of modern medicine's elaborate research facilities at his disposal, yet he was able to conclude that "Drinking genuine[31] tea helps quench the thirst, aids digestion, checks phlegm, wards off drowsiness, stimulates renal activity, improves eyesight and mental prowess, dispels boredom, and dissolves greasy foods."[32] Gu Yunqing's "nine cures" have been confirmed by modern science. No doubt he was also correct when he affirmed that "One cannot do without tea for a single day."[33]

NOTES

1. Christopher Hibbert, *Les empereurs de Chine*, trans. Isabelle Reinharez (Paris: Éditions du Fanal, 1982), 123.

2. Bai Shouyi, ed., *An Outline History of China* (Beijing: Foreign Languages Press, 1982), 309.

3. Hibbert, *Les empereurs*, 124.

4. Bai Shouyi, *Outline History*, 309.

5. Hibbert, *Les empereurs*, 124.

6. Zhang Binglun, *Ancient China's Technology and Science* (Beijing: Chinese Academy of Sciences, 1983), 332.

7. Ibid.

8. John E. Vollner, E. J. Keall, and E. Nagai-Berthrong, *Silk Roads, China Ships: An Exhibition of East-West Trade* (Toronto: Royal Ontario Museum, 1983), 26–27. See also Chapter 4 of this book.

9. The directors of the Dutch East India Company were called "Heeren XVII," thus their designation in English as Lords Seventeen.

10. Zhang, *Ancient China's*, 333. The scion of an English tea dynasty told me, "during my visits to China I certainly got the feeling that a black tea was around before the Tang Dynasty," an opinion (wishful thinking?) shared by many teamen. Unfortunately, suppositions and feelings are not proof. I suspect the claims of an ancient origin for black tea (like an Indian origin of tea) were born in the minds of teamen anxious to add lustre and prestige to their products.

11. Edward L. Dreyer, *Early Ming China: A Political History, 1355–1435* (Stanford: Stanford University Press, 1982), 206.

12. Franz Michael, *The Origin of Manchu Rule in China* (New York: Octagon Books, 1972), 32.

13. Bai Shouyi, *Outline History*, 333–334. One *jin* = 1.3 lb., or 0.6 kg.

14. Dreyer, *Early Ming China*, 222.

15. Lu Yu, *The Classic of Tea*, trans. Francis Ross Carpenter (Boston: Little-Brown, 1974), 167, note 138. Francis Ross Carpenter feels that flower-scented teas existed prior to the Ming Dynasty based on a poem entitled *Scented Tea* by Pao Ling Hui. Prior to the Ming Dynasty tea, especially imperial teas, had been scented with sweet—hence sticky—juices (notably plum juice) used as a binder in the manufacture of tea and not the flower petals introduced during the Ming Dynasty. Carpenter's interesting note quoted here is noteworthy as it describes a method for manufacturing flower-scented teas during the Ming Dynasty:

> Tea was scented by placing layers of flowers between layers of tea. After it was heated the flowers could be sifted out. The flowers most used for scenting tea include: (1) Rose; (2) Plum; (3) Jasmine (a) *Jasminum sambac*; (b) *Jasminum*

paniculatum; (4) *Aglaia odorata* (also used for incense after having been filtered from tea); (5) Orange; and (6) Gardenia. For most of the above the ratio was about 40 lbs. of flowers to 100 lbs. of tea.

16. The origin of the word "orange" in the expression "Orange Pekoe" is uncertain. Mr. Robert Dick suggests that " 'Pekoe' derives from Chinese and 'orange' may as well. Possibly it refers to the orange color of some brewed teas or to the orange tip found on some Indian, Sri Lanka, or Indonesian teas." In the Catalog of Mariage Frères, Paris, it is suggested " 'orange' derived from the Dutch *oranje* meaning 'royal.' " Perhaps it is derived from the Tamil *naru*, meaning "fragrant," since the Chinese themselves always said "fragrant tea." In the bastardized trade language of the Asian seas this became known to European traders as "orange pekoe," in other words, "fragrant tender tea."

17. Zhang, *Ancient China's*, 333.

18. Ibid.

19. Elizabeth Longford, *Victoria R. I.* (London: Weidenfield and Nicholson, 1964), 458. None of England's monarchs liked scented tea except Queen Victoria, who "scented" her tea with whiskey.

20. Originally only the petals of the tea rose *Rosa odorata* were used. Like jasmine flowers, tea rose petals were a less expensive substitute for tea flowers. This native Chinese "half-hardy" bush-rose has large tea-scented blossoms, whence the name "tea rose." Unfortunately, petals from tea roses are not always used and some Rose Congous smell like a bouquet of roses instead of tea.

21. Compare the price of scented teas to that of fine name-teas to know whether scenting is used today to enhance or mask tea's taste. *Caveat emptor!*

22. Most Chinese restaurants in Europe and North America were run by "servant class" Chinese, which explains why jasmine tea became "Chinese restaurant tea." There is a trend now toward increasing the choice of teas in many Chinese restaurants.

23. The term "water *just boiling*" is normally found in Chinese sources. Continued boiling causes the water to lose oxygen, imparting a flat taste to a cup of tea.

24. John Blofeld, *L'art chinois du thé*, trans. Josette Herbert (Paris: Dervy-Livres, 1986), 56.

25. These expressions are quoted from Ming Dynasty novels.

26. These expressions are quoted from Ming Dynasty novels.

27. When the first tea arrived in Europe after direct sea-trading links with China had been established in the 1500s, Europeans drank tea from small handleless china cups (*kraaksporselein*) until a clever European porcelain manufacturer put a handle on them in the eighteenth century, thereby creating the European-style teacup. Europeans have shown a remarkable talent for inventing ingenious teapots, strainers, spoons, slop-bowls, and teabags in an effort to prepare tea more easily. Truly astounding teaware has been invented (it would require a separate volume to merely list these inventions) and the quest continues without anyone taking notice of the truly marvelous *zhong*. The French adopted a modified version of the *zhong* called a *tisanière* used to infuse herbal teas, or *tisanes*, but these often lack both a saucer and a handle and are too hot to touch or move about. Curiously, the *tisanière* is not used for drinking tea, which is traditionally drunk from large breakfast bowls or from small handle-bearing teacups à *l'anglaise*. The Germans do not use *zhong*, although they have a marvelous word for it, *Deckeltasse*, (literally, "covered cup"), which is the closest English equivalent to *zhong*. Period *zhong* are now museum pieces, but excellent and reasonably priced modern copies of Ming and Qing

zhong can be bought in specialty shops. The old-style Wade-Giles spelling of *zhong* is *chung*.

28. Quoted from the Ming novel *The Scholars* by Wu Jingzi.

29. Quoted from the Ming novel *The Scholars* by Wu Jingzi.

30. Aleíjos, *T' u-ch' uan, grüne Wonderdroge Tee* (Vienna: Wilhelm Braumüller, Universitäts-Verlagsbuchhandlung GmbH. , 1987), 39.

31. The reprehensible practice of doctoring tea and selling fake tea was a great problem during the Ming Dynasty.

32. Zhang, *Ancient China's*, 334.

33. Ibid.

10

Qing Dynasty

Part I

1644–1800

Chinese dynasties have always fallen from revolutions fomented in the South or invasions from the North. The floundering Ming Dynasty was torn asunder by both.

Abolishing the postal service for economy's sake in 1628 clearly showed that the Ming had spent themselves into oblivion. The economic decline of the bankrupt state sparked widespread social unrest and the discontented descendants of the peasants who had put the Ming on the Dragon Throne rose up to force it off. The Mandate of Heaven had expired for the Ming.

Rankest superstition replaced logic in governing the realm. An exemplary illustration of the Ming paroxysm of lunacy was the ban on smoking in Beijing. The Emperor had dreamed that "fragrant golden leaf" (tobacco), which sounded like "burning Peking" in Chinese, would set the capital ablaze. In violation of his own decree this foolish emperor continued to smoke his opium *huqqa* as a real threat swelled ominously outside the Great Wall a few miles from his palace.[1] The Mandate of Heaven was destined to bemantle the Manchus.

The Manchus were cousins of the Mongols who descended from the Juched tribes that had ruled northern China during the Great Gold (Jin) Dynasty. As tolerant and open-minded as their ancestors, the Manchus were a fusion of various tribes that had intermarried for centuries. Proud of their heritage, each tribe possessed an identifying banner (this explains the term "banner people" often used in referring to the Manchus). There were altogether eight banners, each of which was identified by a specific color of its flag.[2] No doubt due to their varied ancestry the Manchus were obsessed by genealogy, and one of the favorite Manchu pastimes was talking about their forebears. Even Manchu children had a bard's memory and could recite the names of long lists of ancestors. This Manchu obsession with genealogy would later be applied to the classification of tea with equal thoroughness, resulting in one of the most extensive and complicated naming systems ever devised.

The Manchu chieftain Abahai's Manchurian capital Mukden on the eve of the conquest of China resembled the ephemeral tent cities that mushroomed around the fairs and tournaments of Medieval Europe. Fluttering in the harsh northern winds sweeping across the plains were the Manchu tribal banners, the only color and decorative display in Mukden. The Manchus greatly compensated for this lack of permanence and ostentation once they became China's rulers.

Despite the constant wind, a smoky, foul-smelling cloud always hung low over Mukden. Dust raised by thousands of Manchu horses and sheep made the air barely respirable. One can hardly imagine a less inviting place to drink tea, and most tea drinkers would be revolted by the mixture of tea, salt, and meal—similar to Tibetan Sampa but less consistent—kept hot all night over a wood-burning fire that Manchu soldiers on guard duty around Mukden drank to warm themselves and stay alert. Tea of this kind lent a certain credence to the Chinese disdain of their "barbarian" neighbors to the north.

The Manchus had begun drinking tea long before their second conquest of China. For centuries they had bartered their fine horses for tea. Hoofed stock might at first glance appear to have been the only source of Manchu wealth, yet the desolate Manchurian landscape belied fabulous riches. An abundance of lumber and gold, both of which the Middle Kingdom lacked, were valuable trade items, but growing in Manchuria—one of the few places where it thrived—was a rare, magical plant for which the Chinese were willing to pay several times its weight in gold: fabled ginseng.[3]

The history of ginseng is as exciting as that of tea, again illustrating the risks men will take, even braving their lives, to obtain the rare and precious. The smuggling and doctoring of ginseng echoes the illicit practices perpetrated in the tea trade, and no doubt the contraband of both was controlled behind the scenes by the same ambitious and unscrupulous mandarins.

Manchu leaders of the seventeenth century knew how to exact the full value of their precious ginseng, trading it for expensive Tianjin carpets and tea. The tea preferred by the Manchus was black tea. Although their immense trading profits enabled them to easily obtain the finest green teas, after a century of rule in China where the world's best green teas were theirs by right of conquest, they continued to prefer black tea. Why?

The first clue to elucidating the Manchu preference for black tea and solving the greater mystery of black tea's origin is provided by European travelers to Manchuria. These individuals often mistook cups of black tea for ginseng because infusions of each are so similar that it is difficult to tell them apart just by looking at the brew. However, ginseng's intense aroma and taste were unmistakable and took some getting used to.

Whereas the Chinese preferred "jade green" tea resembling the precious jade they highly valued, the Manchus liked ginseng-colored black tea resembling precious ginseng. Evidence strongly favors the possibility that black tea was developed precisely because its brew was so similar to that of ginseng.

China's Mandate of Heaven was conferred on the Manchus in 1644 after the suicide of the last Ming emperor, thus ushering in the final imperial dynasty to rule China. Ever mindful of the importance of a name, the Manchus at first considered naming their dynasty the "Second Gold (Jin) Dynasty" but decided it sounded too brassy, opting instead for *Qing*, meaning "Pure."

In a goodwill gesture to ingratiate the new dynasty the Manchus wisely decided to abolish the centuries-old tea tax since tea was a necessity like rice. Ironically, when the Manchus lifted the tea tax in China European governments for the first time began taxing it.

China had absorbed the Tang and Mongol conquerors, but Manchu assimilation would never be total. At first the Manchus showed a ready and rapid adoption of the Chinese language, Chinese food, and Chinese manners. Manchu women especially aped Chinese women's ways and began to fard their faces, bow to their husbands, and eat in separate rooms from the men. Heretofore Manchu women had lived on a socially equal footing with Manchu men, eating at the same table and making conversation as the menfolk ate. Their acceptance of the self-effacing, subservient Confucian manner of Chinese women is puzzling—unless, considering the important role women played in Manchu dynastic history, the adoption of Confucian attitudes of obedience was in appearance only. The wholesale adoption of Chinese ways did have its limits, and in 1664 among the legal statutes in the *Code of the Great Qing* the Emperor forbade Manchu women to bind their feet like Chinese women did. However, stylistic influences were exerted in both directions as witnessed by the Chinese wearing of Manchu-style garments buttoning down the front instead of along the sides, and the wearing of the Manchu queue, the *bianzi* or tress of hair.

Throughout the over 250 year duration of the Qing Dynasty Manchu tribal banners symbolized Manchu pride and power. There was no Manchu refusal to sinicize, but it is also true they kept their identity as Manchus alive, a necessary requisite to imposing foreign rule in China. As if Beijing were not close enough to the Manchu homeland, when the dreamlike Baroque extravaganza Summer Palace was constructed it was built outside the Great Wall in Manchuria, where the Imperial Court spent six months of every year. There in the Manchu homeland were all important European ambassadors received by the Emperor. Even 150 years after the conquest of China the Manchu identity was still so pronounced that Aeneas Anderson who accompanied Lord Macartney to China in 1793 could differentiate between the Manchus and the Chinese on sight.

It has been pointed out that a marked preference for black tea was peculiar to the Manchus. The Manchu beverages black tea and ginseng rivaled drinks made from milk. Like the Mongols, the Manchus had a particular fondness for equine milk and they washed down their meals of greasy lamb with a popular milk-wine called *kumis* or the more potent milk-cognac called *arrak*. They added mare's milk to their tea, as had the Mongols.[4]

Long before their second accession to the Dragon Throne, perhaps as early as the Tang Dynasty, the Manchus had begun drinking black tea with milk, a tea that can be justifiably called Manchu-style tea. In 1793 Anderson was surprised that Emperor Qianlong "drank a tea mixture that would little please the Chinese, since the Emperor's tea was infused with as much milk as water."[5] A continued preference for tea with milk is an example of the steadfast Manchu adherence to "banner traditions" throughout the Qing Dynasty.

Manchu-style milk-tea had astounding repercussions; in fact, it became the most popular tea outside of China. Indians owe their tea industry to the English, but the "white tea" immensely popular in India is one prepared exactly like Emperor Qianlong's, which had been introduced along the Coromandel Coast during the seventeenth century. Following the publication of a description of the Dutch Embassy of Captain Moor Mautzuiker, Peter de Goyer, and Jacob de Keyser to China on August 8, 1656, which spoke of adding milk to tea, the novel *Melkthee* appeared at fairs in Holland and Friesland. From there it gained the rest of Europe.[6] In Louis XIV's France the Marquise de Sévigné in one of her famous *Letters* to her daughter on October 4, 1684, recommended drinking tea with both milk and sugar. Parisians following the new fashion mistakenly called tea with milk *thé à la chinoise*, or "Chinese-style tea," when it was actually *thé à la manchoue*, or "Manchu-style tea."

Confusion, errors, and misunderstandings were common in the first decades following the great voyages of discovery. The curious English custom of putting milk into the teacup before the tea dates back to the seventeenth century, when the first trading contacts with Manchu China began. Englishmen assumed tea had to be drunk with milk (because of the Dutch *Melkthee*?) and it seemed logical that the delicate, extremely costly china teacups would break if boiling water were poured directly into them. So cold milk was put into the cup first and has been ever since, despite reasonable arguments to the contrary.

The tea sent to Europe was part of a grand Manchu scheme for an empire based on trade. Beginning in the seventeenth century whole cargoes of precious Chinese goods were literally shoved onto European ships and by 1700 Europe was awash with unsold wares. Porcelain that was formerly so rare flooded already saturated markets, causing a large number of bankruptcies. To make matters worse, the Germans discovered the secret of manufacturing porcelain and added their own wares to the glutted market. Soon thereafter Austria, Italy, France, and England produced porcelain but no European country could produce the tea to fill the porcelain teacups. Throughout the eighteenth century tea would supplant both porcelain and silk to become China's chief export product.

An astounding rise in tea consumption in northern Europe curiously coincided with the closing of China's borders to Europeans during one of the periodic xenophobic seizures that gripped eighteenth-century China. The Manchus had decreed that no man could enter the Celestial Empire unless specifically invited, a law punishable by death. Only "black priest" Jesuits were allowed the special privilege of residing and traveling freely within China; all other Europeans were "quarantined" in coastal ports. In the 1720s even the Jesuit "foreign devils" were expelled and a "bamboo curtain" was drawn across Manchu China. Despite the Chinese blackout—or perhaps prompted by it—Attiret's dissertation on Chinese gardens appeared in 1749. This work strongly influenced Sir William Temple and Sir William Chambers in their design of English gardens. Another book, Walter's best-selling *Voyages of Admiral Anson*, appeared in 1748. It fueled the vogue of *chinoiseries* that inspired Chippendale and influenced European styles in the last half of the eighteenth century.[7] The crescending wave of China-interest caused by these books coupled with Fielding's anti-gin campaign sparked a renewed demand for things Chinese, particularly tea. One can properly speak of a tea craze in England in the 1740s and 1750s when tea sales rose dramatically. Thereafter demand for tea seemed to increase geometrically.

Porcelain manufacturers in both China and Europe welcomed and encouraged the tea craze because each new tea drinker needed a new set of teaware. Porcelain was so fragile that it constantly broke, requiring replacement by still more porcelain. In addition, ladies vied with each other to own the most exquisite teaware, changing tea services with the changing fashions. This change was especially noticeable in the pear, round, and lantern shapes of eighteenth-century teapots.[8]

Foreign tea sales represented a very profitable crop indeed, for China's rulers, financing in part the wasteful luxury of the Imperial Court. Truly, words cannot capture the opulence of the Qing Dynasty, the most astonishingly decadent civilization in the entire history of humanity.[9] Emperor Qianlong (ruled 1736–1795) furnished a multitude of extravagant examples of wanton luxury, yet perhaps the best illustration concerns the Emperor's Pekinese dogs. Since the feet of the Emperor as "Son of Heaven" should never touch the ground, Qianlong reasoned that the paws of his dogs should not either. Exquisite cloisonné cages hung with silk curtains were outfitted with wheels so whenever Emperor Qianlong took the air in the palace gardens he could be accompanied by his favorite dogs, pulled by a eunuch beside the Imperial litter.[10]

An example often cited in Europe to show the wealth of the mandarins concerns the Emperor's *Hoppo*, or viceroy, in Canton. He had amassed such legendary riches that he was able to pay an astounding £97,000 for his mansion, whereas George III of England had paid £28,000 for Buckingham House (later Buckingham Palace) and was denounced as "profligate."[11]

The dream of all Chinese was to have a grand funeral and fortunes were spent in gaudy, ostentatious displays of mourning. Burial rites derived from millennia-old traditions reaching back to the first Chinese. In the last hours before death a person's journey into the netherworld was prepared by attendants who collected money, tea, sweets, and salted and preserved vegetables. They placed these in a small red bag, which was put into the mouth when the person expired. Those who could afford it had a giant "celestial food" pearl put into their mouths. Tea and food were placed in costly hereditary jars and were buried with the deceased to provide for a comfortable afterlife.

The deceased could not be left without tea, and neither could those attending the funeral. An idea of the splendor of Qing China can be seen in Hsi Fang's preparations to keep the Ning Mansion in tea during a wake related in *A Dream of Red Mansions*. After the servants' roll had been called each servant entered one-by-one for inspection. Hsi Fang ordered the following:

These twenty divided into two shifts of ten will be solely responsible for serving tea to guests on their arrival and before their departure. These other twenty in two shifts of ten will see to the family's meals and tea. These forty, divided into two shifts, will burn incense, keep oil in the lamps, hang up curtains, watch the coffin, offer sacrificial rice and tea, and mourn with the mourners. These four will be responsible for the cups, plates and tea things in the pantry. (vol. 1, 187)

Forty-four servants had been assigned to the tea detail!

Chinese mansions employed numerous personnel, usually counting a "respectable" ratio of sixteen servants to each family member. Servants were numerous but they did not do much, each being generally assigned a single task such as those in the Ning Mansion. Although the Tea Master had gone out with cake tea by the time of the Ming Dynasty, the arms and legs of his assistants were still required. Servants were born and died in the same family's service. At different ages they were given different jobs, and when young the first training task they were given was serving tea. Tea boys boiled the tea-water while tea maids measured out the tea leaves, then served the tea and finger foods, then cleaned and cared for the tea things afterwards. Both tea boys and tea maids had permanent tea duty and were on call at all hours of the day and night. In many mansions the first and last duties of a servant were serving tea, and it was quite common to see very old family retainers serving tea assisted by young apprentice servants.

Devoted service carried a sinecure, which is why so many of the old retainers were notoriously lazy and garrulous, constantly grumbling and complaining with impunity. All Chinese servants were noisy, whether it was the sing-song murmur of continuous commentary and jabbering or the boisterous screaming, yelling, and uncontained laughter that so startled and unnerved Europeans.

Life in the great mansions ran quite smoothly because of the big stick held over the servants' heads. Servants in the Ning Mansion, for example, were sure to heed Hsi Fang's warning, "If anything goes wrong, like when a maid serving tea had to fetch rice as well, I shall deal with those concerned."

Chinese masters put up with their servants' moodiness, but any servant caught stealing tea, preparing it badly, or serving it impolitely was swiftly punished. Usually this involved a boxing of the ears or a sound caning, the punishment meted out to servants whose "squeeze" (the amount of pilfering tolerated) had overstepped recognized limits. Manchus complained bitterly of their Chinese servants' stealing; it became a common Manchu proverb that "They would steal the milk out of tea if they could catch hold it it." In order to minimize servants' squeeze the lady of the house distributed supplies and tea as needed, but opportunities for pilfering abounded in the large mansions. China's masses could not afford tea, and servants' selling tea out the back door became a lucrative business.[12]

Beating was a bad punishment but being turned out to beg in the streets was worse. The ominous phrase, "Now go and beg for your tea!" said to all those who were turned out sounded like a death sentence, and in some cases it was.

However, the vast majority of Chinese servants were steadfast and often demonstrated an unwavering loyalty of truly heroic proportions. In 1937 as the Japanese invaders marched toward Nanjing reports of their horrifying savagery[13] preceded them. All who could, fled. One old family retainer in a Nanjing mansion refused to leave, stating nobly, "My family has drunk the tea of this house for five generations and I shall not abandon it now."[14]

While China's upper classes wallowed in idle luxury (many were addicted to opium), waited on hand and foot by legions of servants, most Chinese had to grovel and scrape to earn their tea. The population explosion that occurred in the eighteenth century pushed the number of inhabitants to over 200 million souls, causing a demographic problem that China is still wrestling to control. Crops of tomatoes, sweet potatoes, and corn transplanted from America helped to feed the ever-increasing number of mouths. Unfortunately, the Chinese had also taken to another American import, tobacco, which was definitely smoked for pleasure[15] but also because the Chinese were convinced that it prevented contagious disease.[16] Valuable crop lands were used to grow tobacco (exhausting the soil) and tea instead of food because these crops were big money-makers. Clearly, profit dictated the agricultural priorities of Qing China.

European demand for tea had steadily increased, reaching a colossal 100 thousand tons in 1793. The volume and importance of this trade obliged the monarchs of Europe to send embassies to China seeking trade advantages.[17] The observations made by Aeneas Anderson offer valuable insights into Emperor Qianlong's China and tea usage there. In 1793 Anderson accompanied the British ambassador Earl George Macartney to China.

Lord Macartney and the Englishmen in his party got to taste "Spiritual Leaves Tea made with the night dew from fairy flowers."[18] This was enjoyed by a happy few among the Chinese ruling class, but it proved a rarity for the *misera plebs*. Although tea plantations seemed "to cover all China," Anderson pointed out an ironic paradox: "It is curious that with so much tea there's hardly enough for the lower classes." Here Anderson describes in detail the way the great Chinese masses prepared and drank tea:

The Chinese workers on our junk always asked for the leaves that had been used for our tea. They squeezed the water out and left them to dry in the sun before boiling them for a while. This infusion was put in an earthenware jar and as the liquid diminished boiling water was added. By this method the same leaves could be used to provide tea for several weeks.[19]

The tea-concentrate drunk by the Chinese masses represents the oldest method of preparing tea, a tradition kept alive among the lower classes.

A poignant illustration of the importance accorded tea in China is the curious ritual that Anderson observed in the Dragon Throne Room of the Summer Palace. Although the Emperor himself was absent, court eunuchs ceremoniously made nine prostrated bows (kowtows) to the empty throne before which had been dressed tripods bearing bowls of rice, oil, and tea—all monopolies of the Emperor and revered sources of his great wealth.

Receiving tea from the Emperor—or even being allowed to drink it in his presence—was viewed as an exceptional mark of favor. This was demonstrated when General Zhou Hui returned victorious after a military expedition to Tibet and the Emperor had him served a cup of "fragrant tea." The expression "fragrant tea" is as vague as "tasty tea," and one can only suppose the general's tea had been scented with tea flowers, which Anderson reported "give the most pleasant taste." Or possibly it was the famous *Fujian Wuyi* (Bohea) tea described by Anderson as "having black leaves and a yellow infusion lacking bitterness. Even the flowers are used and the Jesuits complain of its price" (193).

If receiving tea reflected favorably on the Emperor's mood, then what can be concluded by the fact that the august Son of Heaven served Ambassador van Braam wine and Ambassador Macartney tea? Was the tea offered to Macartney *Mao Cha*, made from the tenderest leaves on the branch reserved as Imperial Tribute Tea? Because the Chinese considered Lord Macartney a mere servant from a vassal state, the tea served him would not have been one reserved for the Emperor's personal use.

The Emperor gave the men accompanying Lord Macartney gifts of fine velvet, satin, silk, and "a great quantity of the best tea in the country, compacted solid, having the form and size of a Dutch cheese weighing about five pounds."[20] Unfortunately, Anderson did not mention what kind of tea the imperial gift was or where it had been grown. This is characteristic of Anderson, who gives many hints and clues but frustratingly little detail.

When the Emperor sent gifts to the King of England on April 21, 1806, among them were "four boxes of Spring Tea, and four rolls of Pu'er Tea."[21] Pu'er tea from Yunnan province was already highly prized in the Ming Dynasty. It was a forbidden Imperial Tea domain and trespassers were punished by death, although the tea could be bought legally at the foot of the mountain.[22]

After leaving the Summer Palace Lord Macartney's embassy traveled in regal style along the Imperial Canal down the entire length of China to Canton. Tea was a courtesy drink served to the Englishmen as a refreshment wherever they went, and mandarins often gave them gifts of precious tea.[23]

Anderson mentioned without naming the "covered bowl where tea infuses between the cup and the lid"—the *zhong*—which by then was used almost exclusively in homes, teahouses, and in the Imperial Palace. Etiquette in Qing China required a host to serve every visitor a *zhong* of tea upon arrival no matter what his condition or business. By the eighteenth century the former custom of serving a parting cup of tea had been abandoned except in a few refined, old-fashioned mansions or during wakes and funerals. Already in the Ming Dynasty visitors knew their interview with a mandarin had ended when a second cup of tea was not offered. In the Qing Dynasty the visitor's cue to leave was signaled when a mandarin raised his *zhong* to his lips a second time. Startled Europeans were taken aback when the mandarin touched the *zhong* a second time and servants began screaming to bring the visitor's outer garments and ready his sedan-chair.

Anderson also reported his surprise that the "Chinese drink their tea without sugar because they never put any in tea."[24]

Europeans visiting China shared Anderson's surprise because almost everyone in Europe did sugar their tea. The Jesuit Attiret was among the first to observe that the Chinese drank tea without sugar. Attiret had even underscored the phrase to emphasize the point. Sugar was, however, added to tea in a few Chinese regions, for example in the Bohea (Wuyi) Mountains where a peculiar shaped sugar-spoon was used to stir the yellow rock sugar until it dissolved. Generally, sugaring tea was an exception in China. In fact, the refrain "Tea without sugar like the Chinese" was often voiced as a political statement in the nineteenth century when Europeans boycotted sugar to protest against slavery.

Another surprise to Europeans visiting China was to see the Chinese drinking tea all day long. Englishmen were accustomed to drinking tea only twice a day, in the morning and in the evening. While Englishmen might take tea with their food, the Chinese almost never did, preferring wine instead. Most of the liquid taken at a Chinese meal actually came from the soup that was traditionally served at the end of each meal.

After the meal a *zhong* of tea was customarily served, but it was considered bad manners—even unhealthy—to gulp down this tea meant only for rinsing the mouth. The Jade Boy in *A Dream of Red Mansions* made this mistake and was harshly upbraided. Tea meant to be drunk was served at least thirty minutes *after* a meal.

By the end of the eighteenth century there existed such a wide divergence between European and Chinese tea manners that the only common denominator was a shared opinion of tea as a social beverage.

Scenting tea with flowers had begun with the Ming, and jasmine tea remained (and remains) a favorite drink before and after meals. In addition to existing flower-scented teas, during the Qing Dynasty fruit-scented teas appeared. The novel exotic fruits *arbustus* (strawberries), mango, and litchi were used to flavor tea. Small, sweet Sichuan tangerines had once been used to scent tea, but when they proved too expensive they were replaced by the cheaper bergamot (*Citrus bergamia*), creating the famous "Earl Grey" tea that is still popular today.

Anderson and other Europeans "invited" into Qianlong's China were only shown and told what the Chinese desired. When Anderson saw "thick columns of smoke" he knew "a porcelain factory must lie nearby,"[25] but never was he allowed to see one in operation. Questions not meant to be answered were met with blank, uncomprehending stares. Tea plantations spread out to the horizon on each side of the Imperial Canal but tea harvesting, processing, and even transportation were purposely kept from view. When information was volunteered it had to be treated circumspectly.

Once a Chinese man spontaneously offered to explain how tea was picked. He told Anderson, "Tea growers anger the monkeys living in the branches of tea trees. Out of revenge the monkeys tear off branches and throw them on the ground. In this way tea harvesters only have to pick them up."

Anderson truthfully admitted he had not witnessed the monkey-harvest himself although he nonetheless accepted the story as fact. All of Europe read Anderson's book and the monkey tea-picking legend found its way to the West. This story had a particular appeal and fascination for the Victorians, no doubt due to the furor raised by Darwin's theory of evolution. For over a century children's schoolbooks contained the story, and several generations of adults were convinced tea was picked by monkeys.

The trade advantages Lord Macartney had sought were courteously, but definitely, denied. Macartney's embassy was not totally unsuccessful, however, since it had enabled the capital stock of the East India Company to reach £6,000,000, with an additional million subscribed at 200 percent.[26] Moreover, it had started Englishmen thinking. A single tea tree brought to England in 1768 by John Ellis growing in the Kew Gardens helped germinate the idea that England's colonies might produce tea for the British Empire.[27]

NOTES

1. Fu Lo-Shu, *A Documentary Chronicle of Sino-Western Relations, 1644–1820* (Tucson: University of Arizona Press, 1966), 518–519, note 84.

2. Bai Shouyi, ed., *An Outline History of China* (Beijing: Foreign Languages Press, 1982), 358.

3. Lu Yu, *The Classic of Tea*, trans. Francis Ross Carpenter (Boston: Little, Brown, 1974), 155, note 16. "Tea may have been second only to ginseng in the number of recipes in which it figures even in early China."

4. W.J.F. Jenner, *Memories of Loyang* (Oxford: Clarendon Press, 1981), 129.

5. Aeneas Anderson, *Relation du voyage de Lord Macartney à la Chine*, ed. Gilles Manceron (Paris: Éditions Aubier Montaigne, 1978), 134.

6. Fu Lo-Shu, *Documentary Chronicle*, 18–19.

7. Attiret was a Jesuit priest who is best remembered for the portraits he painted of the Manchu Court. His work is published in *Lettres édifiantes et curieuses de Chine par des missionaires Jésuites, 1702–1776*. Isabelle and Jean-Louis Vissière (Paris: Garnier-Flammarion, 1977), 411–429. Commodore Anson went to China on September 21, 1743. See Fu Lo-shu, *Documentary Chronicle*, 175.

8. Hans Herlin, *Das Taschenbuch vom Tee* (Munich: Wilhelm Heyne Verlag, 1980), 83–85. Mr. Herlin has graphically represented the evolution of the teapot in the eighteenth and nineteenth centuries. See also the unsurpassed collection in the Victoria and Albert Museum (London).

9. This is my personal opinion, although a strong case can be made for the sultans of the Ottoman Empire and the Moghul rulers of India.

10. Christopher Hibbert, *Les empereurs de Chine* (Paris: Éditions du Fanal, 1982), 155.

11. P. Colquhoun, *A Treatise on the Wealth, Power, and Resources of the British Empire in Every Quarter of the World* (London: Joseph Mawman, 1815), 201. "By an act also of the 15th of January, Buckingham House was settled on the Queen, which had been previously purchased for £28,000, to which is to be added £72,627 for enlarging, embellishing and improving what is now called the Queen's Palace. This expenditure produced a great clamour in the country." Aeneas Anderson put the figure at £21,000.

12. Perhaps the English followed the Chinese example because at the same time, despite England's tea glut, the English lower classes could not easily afford tea and resorted to buying smuggled, doctored, and "Once used!" tea leaves sold out the back door by servants. One wonders if the famous "Once used!" tea leaves had been those normally used by footmen to keep the carpets clean and fresh.

13. This example of modern barbarity is known as the "Rape of Nanking," a violent, senseless act of inhumanity that has never been forgotten, forgiven, or avenged. Anna Louise Strong in her astounding book *One-Fifth of Mankind* (New York: Modern Age Books, 1938) made this shocking revelation: "Crashing into the picture of kindly, courteous civilians comes an item in one of the leading Japanese newspapers (*Osaka Mainichi Shimbun*, February 9, 1938), the cheerful account of the "Slay-1000-Persons Contest!" Subaltern Noda, with the Japanese army in China, made a wager with Subaltern Sakii that he would be the first to kill one hundred persons. He found this so easy and agreeable that the wager was raised to one thousand. "In North China," wrote the gleeful Noda, "the pleasure of the game was minimized by the fatigue of chasing the enemy, but in Central China one can kill and kill without much trouble. . . . Just before I entered the city of Nanking [Nanjing] I had slain 105 persons. . . . Afterwards, in the rounding-up battles, I took another 253. The slaying was quite easy, but one must yet indulge in a hearty massacre to be really satisfied. . . . I have now, entered into an agreement with Subaltern Sakii to slay one thousand." The account of this "game" in the Japanese newspaper was endorsed by many readers' comments of approval" (14). The Japanese general responsible has not served a single day in prison. George Orwell remarked on the horror story about the Japanese at Nanjing in 1942. "There is not the slightest doubt about the behavior of the Japanese in China," *Essays and Journalism, 1940–1943* (London: Book Club Associates, 1981), 597–598.

14. Anecdote told to me by A. Chung Sze, who kindly permitted its inclusion here.

15. Fu Lo-Shu, *Documentary Chronicle*, 518, notes 84–85. "The practice of smoking tobacco mixed with opium was probably first introduced into China from Java by the Dutch. The Chinese in Java often smoked opium when they were not working. They learned how to smoke it there because it was considered a means of entertaining or encouraging sociability. . . . Opium can prevent people from being attacked by malaria, cholera, and other tropical disease. Probably for this reason the Dutch introduced the use of opium in Formosa from where it gained Amoy and the rest of China".

16. The earliest finely shaped, four-inch Elizabethan clay pipes were called "plague pipes" in the belief tobacco would ward off the bubonic plague.

17. Earl Swisher, *China's Management of the American Barbarians* (New York: Octagon Books, 1972), 131. The first U.S. diplomatic mission was that of Caleb Cushing from November 15, 1843 to December 14, 1844. For an account of this mission see pages 131–178. Anna Louise Strong (in *One-Fifth of Mankind*) stated that "When Washington was president, the China trade formed one-seventh of all American imports and created the great fleet of clipper ships which made the Yankee sailors the speed kings of the seas. The clever Yankees, knowing the Chinese lack of interest in foreign wares, took ice from New England to tropical Canton; Icehouse Street in Hong Kong is a souvenir of those days" (46).

18. Aeneas Anderson, *Relation du voyage de Lord Macartney à la Chine*, ed. Gilles Manceron (Paris: Éditions Aubier Montaigne, 1978), 190. The original English title of Anderson's book was *A Journal of an Embassy from the King of Great Britain to the Emperor of China in the Years 1792, 1793, 1794*. Another member of the mission named George Staunton wrote an account entitled *An Authentic Account of the Earl of Macartney's Embassy from the King of Great Britain to the Emperor of China*.

19. Anderson, *Relation*, 67–68.

20. Ibid., 134.

21. Fu Lo-Shu, *Documentary Chronicle*, 367.
22. Lu Yu, *Classic*, 30.
23. Anderson, *Relation*, 195.
24. Ibid., 83.
25. Ibid., 199.
26. Colquhoun, *Treatise*, Appendix, 89.
27. Lu Yu, *Classic*, 41.

11

Qing Dynasty
Part II
1800–1912

The expression "All the tea in China" truly reflected reality at the beginning of the nineteenth century when China—and only China—produced tea. Until the late 1830s the word "China" in the term "China tea" was superfluous since tea was axiomatically Chinese; in fact, no one living at the time of the Napoleonic Wars could have predicted or even conceived the preposterous idea that within a few short, eventful decades the tea world would be turned upside down. China would lose her tea monopoly and thereafter would play a secondary role in the international tea market.

In 1800 China produced the world's tea but the international tea market was firmly controlled by England. Due to its monopoly the powerful British East India Company had held a stranglehold over the commercialization of China's teas from the seventeenth to the nineteenth centuries. Yet the monopoly it enjoyed disserved it in the end, for during the latter part of the eighteenth century the Company was literally being crushed with unsold tea and was close to bankruptcy. This was a consequence of a mountainous accumulation of tea in the Company's London warehouses arising from increased smuggling. When customs duties amounted to "cent. per cent. on the cost," legal tea sales declined. Beginning in 1773 tea sales slipped to 5,559,007 lbs. from an average of 8,075,794 lbs. for the five preceding years.[1] Smuggling was clearly ruining the English company.[2] The immoral steps—and their dire consequences—taken by the East India Company in an effort to stave off bankruptcy will be discussed shortly.

The Company's many problems were further compounded (and England's grasp of the world tea market profoundly affected) by the rapid succession of innovations in transportation during the nineteenth century. The appearance of clipper ships, railroads, and steamships each caused a major readjustment in the tea market. Tea itself would play a leading role in the "Great Game"[3] of British imperial politics. England's aspiration to empire would practically eliminate China from the international tea market by the end of the century.

THE CLIPPER ERA

The Romantic Movement that ushered in the century had its yearning for beauty realized upon the high seas in the tea clippers. The shortlived Clipper Era, roughly spanning the decades from the 1820s to 1860s, provides an exciting chapter in maritime history that left a legacy of truly heroic proportions. Sleek ships laying low in the water crowned with a towering mass of billowing sail,[4] the clippers derived from American blockade runners used during the War of 1812. Designed for speed, literally clipping through the water, these racy replacements of the stodgy East Indiamen were the fastest cargo-carrying ships ever to sail the high seas. Resembling elegant yachts, the clippers' elongated, eye-pleasing lines belied the fact that they were built to carry cargo, and tons of it.[5]

THE OPIUM TRADE

The romance attached to tea clippers masks a shameful *Schattenseite* that tarnished their reputation due to the deeply shocking practice of carrying opium. While the general public's attention was diverted by the much heralded "first tea races" pitting clippers against each other to be the first to dock in London with the spring harvest of China tea, secret cargoes of opium from Turkey and Bengal were smuggled silently into China. Tea clippers transported just as much opium with the same efficiency and rapidity as tea. Thus the degrading appellation "opium clippers" is as appropriate as the term "tea ships," which they were called at the time.

When the Swiss physician Paracelsus (whose real name was Bombast von Hohenheim) recommended the use of "beneficial" opium in 1527, he had no idea what demons he had unleashed.

Opium and the other narcotic members of the opiate family—laudanum, morphine, and heroin—all derive from *Papaver somniferum*, the white-blossomed Oriental cousin of the benign red poppies that are common in European and American grain fields. Arab traders had first brought opium into China during the Tang Dynasty, "but it was seldom used." By the Ming Dynasty the price of opium was "as high as gold" and the Ming Emperor Wanli's early death was due to opium.[6]

Like all drugs opiates are harmful when abused, which is almost always the case because they are highly addictive. Opium's use had been limited until about 1740 when two Englishmen living in India named Wheeler and Watson had the idea of commercializing Bengali opium in China. Regrettably, the first illicit English shipment of opium met tremendous success.[7]

Opium importation had been illegal from the very beginning. Prohibited by the Chinese law of 1727, it was repeatedly banned by even harsher laws, which indicates that the potential destructiveness of the drug was fully recognized.[8] An Imperial Decree of April 4, 1810 stated, "Opium has a very violent effect. When an addict smokes it, it rapidly makes him extremely excited and he is capable of doing anything he pleases. But before long it kills him. Opium is a prison, undermining our good customs and morality."[9]

Robert Clive's unification of India in 1757 on behalf of the British East India Company was a boon to the opium trade, which by then was operating with the complete agreement—even encouragement—of London. As Gideon Hall Chase pointed out in 1879 in his book *Dishonourable Company*, Bengal-grown opium was cultivated under the watchful eye of the Company's Opium Department and its Opium Agent, Deputy Opium Agent, and Sub-Deputy Opium Agent, who worked hand-in-hand with the Resident, District Revenue Collector, Magistrate, Judge, Civil Surgeon, and military officers of the Queen's Regiments. Perhaps the most prestigious of all civil service posts in India was that of Commissioner of Patna, where the best opium grew. An Englishman whose surname was followed by the coveted letters I.C.S. (Indian Civil Service) as late as the 1930s headed the Departments of Opium and Salt.[10]

After harvesting and processing the opium was sent under guard to Calcutta, where it was auctioned off by the Company to wholesale merchants for export. The presence of many bidders drove the price up, and because opium prices were high tea prices were kept artificially high. Furthermore, since opium was carried and traded between Calcutta and Canton in the ships of more than 6,000 "Free Traders," the Company felt it had disengaged itself of all responsibility in the drug traffic.

Since the beginning of the China trade Europeans had paid for tea and other Chinese goods in silver, the only commodity the Europeans possessed that the Chinese wanted. Chinese shroffs (from the Arabic *sarraf*) who had the double function of banker and assayer "chopped" with ideogram seals (chop marks) each silver Spanish and Mexican "Carolus" dollar received from the Europeans. They also oversaw the minting of *sycee* (fine silk) silver nicknamed "Chinese shoes" because the ingots had been molded in forms resembling shoe soles.[11] The trade balance so favored China that the British East India Company tottered on the brink of bankruptcy, literally exsanguinated of its silver lifeblood with mountains of unsold tea piled high in its London warehouses.

Opium was worth £500,000 to the British, providing a whopping one-seventh of the total revenue for British India. Had it not been for silver profits from opium sales the English could have ill afforded their Indian colony. Opium not only financed the Indian possessions, it was used literally to defend them as well. Each sepoy carried a small tin box containing Patna opium pills; when each soldier took half a pill washed down with a little cold tea before a battle, it made them "fight like tigers." In China opium pills bore the engaging name "Golden Pill."[12]

Opium paid for the Company's tea purchases, while the £3 to £4 million annual revenue obtained "painlessly" by the nominal Tea Tax paid by British tea-drinkers paid half the cost of maintaining the Royal Navy. Without opium there would have been no tea, no Royal Navy, and no British Raj.[13]

Opium was a product addicts could not do without. The growing number of Chinese addicts required an ever-increasing amount of opium to satisfy their addiction. Soon the British were in a position to demand payment for opium in silver specie in a complete reversal of the trade wheel.

One reads in Chinese history books today, "While the British colonialists were busy selling opium not only did millions of Chinese lose their health or their will to live a constructive life, but large quantities of silver also flowed out of the country."[14]

Opium was destined principally but not exclusively for China. Many Englishmen living in India were constantly "banged up to the eyes with opium" (from *bhang*, an intoxicating infusion of India hemp), which prompted India's Governor-General Warren Hastings to call opium "a pernicious article of luxury which ought not to be permitted but for purposes of foreign commerce only." This was a clear warning that opium could become a more serious problem in Europe and America, where sordid opium dens existed in London's Seven Dials and New York's Five Points sections. Saint-John de Crèvecoeur was amazed to discover when he visited Nantucket in 1776 that "all the inhabitants were opium addicts, including the sheriff."[15] Ann Randolph, sister of Thomas Jefferson's son-in-law, was an "unfortunate opium addict," and we are astounded by a letter penned by Jefferson's daughter in which she says she had increased Jefferson's nightly dose of laudanum "by 100 drops." This statement indicates that Jefferson himself was probably addicted,[16] since it only required six drops of opium for Paquita to render her duenna unconscious.[17] The opiate-based "Godfrey's Cordial" was routinely prescribed for sick children. Could some of the "Romantic pallor" and bizarre "drunken" behavior cited in period annals be accounted for by opium addiction?[18]

Nowhere was the abuse of opium more pernicious than in China. After the death of Emperor Qianlong the golden age of Qing China ended and from then on there seemed to be no way of stemming the tide of opium. Despite more stringent laws against opium importation passed on May 2, 1815,[19] the number of Chinese addicts continued to rise alarmingly. An Imperial Decree stated:

> Opium spreads deadly poison. Rascals and bandits indulge in it and cannot do without it even for a second. They do not save their own earnings for food and clothes, but instead exchange their money for the pleasure of this narcotic. Not only do they willingly bring ruin upon their own lives, but they also persuade friends to follow their example. There is no doubt that opium will harm the morality of our people.[20]

Many children between ten and fifteen years of age were addicted and it was not uncommon to find addicts who smoked 200 pipes a day—an astonishing four ounces. Special "opium shops" catered to addicts, openly displaying a piece of yellow paper that had served to filter opium extract (the dried juice of the opium poppy) in defiance—or rather, with the connivance—of the Chinese authorities and police. A reeking odor suffocated anyone entering the opium dens, lighted only by the dim flames of small spirit lamps made by Americans whose clipper ships carried them by the tens of thousands to China. As many as twenty smokers were stretched out in lifeless languor on bamboo slats (the horizontal position was reportedly "necessary for proper enjoyment"), a cup of tea within easy reach to extinguish their burning thirst. Tea is a natural antidote to opium but most addicts had gone past the stage where it was effective. Quite often the teacup was filled with opium tea: Millions of Chinese addicts constantly drank opium tea, which was concocted by brewing in boiling water the crusts of opium that had accumulated inside the bowls of opium pipes.[21]

Thousands of pipes of opium accompanied by as many cups of opium tea often resulted in madness. The Dutch governor-general of Java was forced to place policemen at the doors of all opium shops with orders to *kill on sight* any demented opium addict who tried to leave.[22]

Robert Fortune was a fearless man, yet he mentions seeing in a teahouse in China "people who had an appearance which did not produce a favourable impression on one. They were evidently opium-smokers from the sallow colour of their cheeks, probably gamblers and altogether such characters as one would rather avoid than be on intimate terms with."[23]

Wealthy addicts (of which there were many) rarely visited the sordid opium shops, preferring the comfortable privacy of rooms in their houses reserved especially for opium smoking. These private dens were luxuriously decorated with beautifully embroidered silk wall-hangings and intricately carved lacquer couches. Fellow addicts were invited to opium parties and it was not uncommon to see bodies clad in fine silks sprawled inert on the cushioned luxury of a *kang*.

It is significant that the period of Victorian literature opened with Thomas de Quincey's *Confessions of an Opium Eater* (1856) (his son-in-law was addicted to opium pills[24]) and ended with one of literature's most famous addicts, a detective named Sherlock Holmes. Yet the average Victorian simply chose to close his eyes to the opium traffic and pretend it did not exist, even calling the conflict now known as the Opium War the "Burmese War." This same Victorian would look shocked and shrug off as "humbug" if he was told that opium financed the British Empire, provided his high standard of living, and paid for all the tea he and his countrymen drank. The revenue that tea brought into the British Exchequer averaged £3,300,000 yearly. Tea from China alone provided about one-tenth of the total revenue of England and the entire profits of the East India Company.[25] The same Englishman would have denied as preposterous the very idea that the East India Company was executing a well thought out plan to addict the Chinese to opium and the British to tea.

That tea itself was then considered a drug can be seen in the statement appearing in the *Canton Monitor*, "tea remains a *drug* on the London market" (November 1835). By law the East India Company had to keep a year's stock of tea in its London warehouses "lest the froward and turbulent urban populations of our island might even temporarily be deprived of what has become to them increasingly a staple of existence" (ibid.). It was feared the "addicted populace" might revolt if deprived of tea. In a letter to John Abel Smith, James Matheson wrote,

It is worthy of consideration, whether as tea is such a necessity of life in England ... the British Government will not in the event of hostilities with China prefer to connive at the export of teas through foreigners rather than by establishing a blockade, cut off the supplies to the distress of our turbulent home population, not to mention the defalcation of the revenue.[26]

The drugs of tea and opium made the English and Chinese populations mutually dependent as tea and opium became indissociable in the diabolically ingenious trade scheme devised by the East India Company.

Ironically, the Company's monopoly of England's tea imports was jeopardized by the Free Traders, the very people the Company needed to carry opium to China in order to keep from soiling itself in the drug traffic. Open trade finally forced Parliament in April 1834 to revoke the tea monopoly the Company had enjoyed for over two centuries. A year later on November 23, 1835 the *Canton Monitor* observed that the

> ready [tea] supplies continued to overhang and depress the prices at the auctions. . . . Tea is now a glut on the London market owing to the circumstances of throwing open that trade to all comers. The great number of vessels which resorted to this port [Canton] to take on cargoes of tea at the ridiculously inflated prices the brokers were demanding merely combined to drive down each other's profits at the London auctions. Now these same shippers cannot prevail upon wholesalers to take their teas at any price. Stocks of tea are on hand, it is estimated, which will supply all conceivable wants of our domestic populations for three years.

Keeping the tea glut in mind, the vast temperance campaigns launched in Europe and America in the 1830s and 1840s (orchestrated by the East India Company?) appear less surprising. During large and often hysterical temperance meetings (such as those described by Charles Dickens in *The Pickwick Papers*) people drank an astonishing number of cups of tea. George Cruikshank's famous caricatural series *The Bottle* artfully illustrated the teetotal campaign. The Victorian vogue for afternoon tea-parties began at this time and soon thereafter the first tearooms opened. A concerted—and successful—effort had been launched to make the English population drink more tea because the flooding of China with opium caused England to be flooded with tea.

Small chests of sticky opium balls smuggled into China paid for all tea exports and determined the amount of tea exported. The *Lin Tin Bulletin and River Bee* on Wednesday, July 18, 1838 (Vol. 1, No. 15) observed, "As the legitimate trade in tea is so inextricably bound up with the clandestine traffic in drugs, it may be anticipated that any dislocations felt now in the import of opium will be reflected some months hence in constrictions and insolvencies in the tea-trade, especially as regards the exports of our British cousins."

In order to know what was happening in the tea market one had to keep an eye on the opium traffic.

America was far from blameless in the opium trade, and its official "Open Door Policy" was indeed "hitchhiking imperialism." After Independence an American ship of 212 tons named the *Columbia* was sent on its maiden voyage to China by Boston merchants. Captained by the Rhode Islander Robert Gray, the *Columbia* followed the same course taken earlier by Captain Cook's *Resolution*. It ferried sea otter skins from Nootka Sound that were exchanged in Canton for tea and other Chinese goods.[27]

Captain Cook was the earliest to realize that one could make a great fortune trading American furs for tea in Canton. John Jacob Astor made his money this way.[28] Although the legitimate trade returned a handsome profit in silk, porcelain, lacquer furniture, and tea, the lure of even greater opium profits proved irresistible and several American traders began dealing in opium, often rivaling the British. With their rapid clipper ships Americans enjoyed a virtual monopoly of Turkish opium, misleading many Chinese into believing that Turkey was part of the United States. Jefferson's decision to send in the marines at Tripoli had the higher purpose[29] of asserting U.S. rights to freely sail the world's oceans but also put an end to harassment and kidnapping of U.S. ships and sailors by Barbary pirates, thereby insuring a safe passage for U.S. clippers fully laden with Turkish opium bound for China.[30] After Parliament opened British ports to ships of all nationalities in 1834, those of the "Flowery Flag Republic"[31] began buying Indian opium at the Calcutta auction as well.[32]

After 1820 the fur trade ceased to be a factor in the Far East and increasingly Americans became implicated in trading in "opium, the dirt used in smoking."[33]

In the well-appointed drawing rooms of Americans living in Canton and Macao a permanent fixture was the raised, elegantly wrought silver stand-dish in which were invariably found sweet, chewy "Turkish Delights," or *lukums*. Yet within the dank holds of the same ships bringing this delicacy was the opium that killed tens of thousands of Chinese. None of this trade touched America directly, since "Americans smuggled opium from Smyrna, Turkey to Canton but not from America."[34] How many tea fortunes had actually been made handling opium? Who were the "rather stuffy Victorian families" obliged to maintain a "deep conspiracy of silence about the source of the family income?"[35]

No one side bears total responsibility for the opium trade; there is sufficient guilt for all. China's Manchu rulers always cast a wary eye on

South China's tea fortunes and viewed the opium traffic as a way to reduce the riches of Canton merchants and put South China to sleep, thereby lessening the threat of revolt.

Opium addiction in China would eventually attain monstrous proportions, alarming even the mandarins in Beijing who had once encouraged it. *The Lin Tin Bulletin and River Bee* (Vol. 2, No. 14) listed the following opium imports:

Season	Quantity
1700	200 chests
1800	5,000 chests
1820	6,000 chests
1830	17,000 chests
1838	40,000 chests

During the same period Chinese sources[36] give the following opium imports:

1787	200 chests
1800	2,000 chests
1820	5,147 chests
1821	7,000 chests
1824	12,639 chests
1834	21,785 chests
1837	39,000 chests
1850	50,000 chests

Depending on the source, figures for the opium trade vary widely. This is to be expected since the opium traffic was illegal.[37]

The volume of opium smuggled into China prompted a thunderous editorial commentary in the *Lin Tin Bulletin* and *River Bee* (Vol. 2, No. 14): "How may a ruler leave his subjects on thrall to a thing, a lump of brown sap? Better to be a man's slave than an object's." The "thrall" was not easily dispelled. Chinese authorities arrested "opium eaters" and their suppliers daily, and the Emperor issued an indignant decree expressing outrage that opium was being smuggled into the Forbidden City.[38]

Despite the risk, "scrambling crabs" and "fast dragons" (names given the small rapid boats ferrying the opium from the Free Traders' ships) were always able to make their opium runs. Ironically, it was the legitimate traders who were the worst affected by the Chinese customs controls because their legitimate cargoes rotted while waiting for official inspection.

Relations between the European traders and the Chinese officials in Canton deteriorated rapidly, approaching a stalemate that proved unprofitable for all but the smugglers. The *Lin Tin Bulletin and River Bee* of October 1838 (Vol. 1, No. 21) explained the "horns of the dilemma":

1. The Chinese Government wishes to extirpate a vicious trade which ruins the health of its subjects and drains its treasury of precious specie.

2. The English Government admits the immorality of the trade but cannot afford to lose its vast profits.

By putting the onus for its suppression on the Chinese Government, saying piously that one sovereign power may not interfere in the internal affairs of another, Britannia has the best of all worlds: she gets the lucre, yet washes her hands of all moral responsibility.

We do not think this can continue.

Indeed, the Chinese struck a bold and justified blow against the opium traffic in March 1839, when Imperial Commissioner Lin Zexu, a folk hero in China today, brashly ordered that all opium in European warehouses be turned over to him. The opium smugglers chose Captain Charles Elliott to represent them. He agreed to surrender 20,291 chests of opium (about half the annual opium imported to China) while "guaranteeing the merchants compensation from the British Government."[39]

Under the watchful eye of Commissioner Lin the confiscated opium chests were counted no less than four times to insure that no theft had occurred. The *Lin Tin Bulletin and River Bee* of May 1839 (Vol. 2, No. 11) explained how this opium was disposed of:

Lin had caused a most ingenious system of trenches and sluices to be dug on the heights of the precipitous island and filled with ash and lime. Into this destructive liquid was hurled the contents of the opium chests. Following the elapse of a period of time, sufficient to permit the reagents to perform their work of dissolution, a flood of sea-water was allowed to flow through the system, reducing the consumed opium to the consistency of a sludge or horrid porridge, and washing it into the receiving sea.[40]

No less than twenty-three days were required just to destroy the confiscated opium. Bai Shouyi contests the manner of destruction saying the opium was burned on Humen Beach. Evidently there is room for conjecture about this incident.

Commissioner Lin's famous opium stand was followed by his equally famous "moral advice" to the young Queen Victoria,[41] who had been only one year on the throne. Lin began with the question, "Where is your conscience?" He thereby artfully put all the blame squarely on the British before he elaborated the Chinese complaints:

Of all that China exports to foreign countries there is not a single thing which is not beneficial to people. Is there a single article from China which has done any harm to foreign countries? Take tea and rhubarb, for example; the foreign countries cannot get along for a single day without them. If China cuts off these benefits with no sympathy for those who are to suffer, then what can the barbarians [i.e., the Europeans] rely upon to keep themselves alive? . . . We can get along without articles coming from outside China that can be used merely as toys. Our Celestial Court lets tea, silk and other goods be shipped without limit and circulated everywhere without begrudging it in the slightest. This is for no other reason but to share the benefit with the people of the whole world.[42]

The Chinese commonly believed that Europeans were absolutely dependent on silk, tea, and rhubarb,[43] and consequently Lin's statement that Europeans "cannot get along for a single day without tea" is a veiled threat. The Chinese actually believed every word in Commissioner Lin's letter, as we will shortly see.

Britain's Prime Minister, Lord Palmerston, found Commissioner Lin's letter so insulting that he promptly called for war. At odds with him was the noted tea-drinker Gladstone, who spoke out strongly against an armed response. Gladstone pointed out that tea, silk, and porcelain *together* were less profitable than opium, which explained why traders sailed the Turkey-India-China route without ever returning to their home ports. He righteously condemned the Opium War, declaring, "a war more unjust in its origin, a war more calculated in its progress to cover this country with permanent disgrace I do not know of. . . . The [British] flag is become a pirate flag to protect the infamous traffic."[44]

Unfortunately, Palmerston carried the day. The Opium War of 1840–1842 began, a war that pitted the might of Imperial China against Imperial Britain.

One of the first acts of war taken by the Chinese was the issuance of a decree by the Emperor placing an embargo on the export of tea and rhubarb. This proved that Commissioner Lin's letter to Queen Victoria had truly reflected the Chinese Court's belief that the English would "immediately capitulate if deprived of these." In this light the great "tea glut" in London can be considered as seige-stocks sufficient to meet the needs of England's "turbulent populace" for three years in the event the Chinese cut off the tea supply.

England's tea merchants and tea-drinkers had no need to worry about a tea shortage. In the absence of China tea, the Australian "tea tree" (*Leptospermum*),[45] whose leaves were already used as a substitute for tea, provided a fair ersatz. More important, just two years before the outbreak of hostilities with China Indian-grown Assam tea had been successfully commercialized in London. The far-reaching British Empire afforded additional commercial possibilities as well. This was noted by P. Colquhoun in 1814:

> I have (says Mr. Percival) in my possession a letter from an officer in the 80th regiment wherein he states that he had found the real tea plant in the woods of Ceylon and of a quality equal to any that ever grew in China, and that it was in his power to point out to Government that means of cultivating it in a proper manner. The vast advantages to be derived from the cultivation of the tea plant in our dominions ought at least to prompt a speedy and vigorous experiment on the subject.[46]

The "vast advantages" of growing tea in England's colonies did not escape notice, as witnessed by the Assam experiment. The Opium War drove home the point that if Britain were to be free of Chinese trade caprices and dependence on Chinese tea it was necessary to produce enough tea in her own colonies to be self-sufficient.

No penury of tea occurred in the West during the Opium War because stocks abroad were great. Assam tea production was increased, but even at the war's apogee enormous amounts of tea continued to be exported from China despite the tea embargo.

Although Canton was closed to the opium traffic the numerous bays and coves along the irregular South China coastline offered numerous possibilities for quickly off-loading or on-loading contraband goods. Opium smuggling was brisk and profits greater than ever because Commissioner Lin had destroyed half a year's supply of opium, and thousands of addicts *en manque* would pay almost any price to obtain the drug that held them in thrall. The *Lin Tin Bulletin and River Bee* of January 1839 (Vol 2, No. 3) related:

At this time the price of drug has fallen by fully half . . . now well below $400 a chest of finest Malwa or Patna opium. The drug-traders can thank Lin for striking a good bargain on their behalf for they could barely sell the drug at a price which would leave them in profit such was the glut and state of the market these last months.

Since the tea trade mirrored the opium traffic it is not surprising that windfall wartime opium profits resulted in a proportionately greater number of tea chests destined for export. Throughout the conflict, in fact, opium deliveries continued unimpeded while fresh stocks of tea were shipped to England.

In March 1841 Captain Elliott arranged a truce that just happened to coincide with the spring tea harvest. During the short break in hostilities the British were able to load cargoes of tea worth £3 million sterling (representing opium profits) with the blessings of their Chinese enemies. However, Captain Elliott's career became a casualty of the Opium War. Palmerston replaced him with Sir Henry Pottinger on August 10, 1841.[47] Pottinger remained to negotiate the Treaty of Nanking.[48]

Chinese irrealism and conceit had actually lead them to play into English hands, since the embargo on tea helped rather than hurt the British. The tea glut in London should have depressed tea prices, but tea's price (like that of any other product) rose when it was difficult to obtain. Since the Chinese had conveniently removed themselves from the international tea market, the price of tea glut tea and Indian-grown tea remained artificially high. This amply rewarded investors in Indian tea plantations and helped to establish the renown of India's teas.

THE OPIUM WAR: THE DÉNOUEMENT

The outcome of the Opium War seemed a foregone conclusion because China's army, although vastly outnumbering the British, was equipped with medieval cut-and-hack weapons unable to match British firepower. Worse even than defeat itself were the humiliating terms of the Treaty of Nanking. These terms obliged the Chinese to (1) pay for the opium that Commissioner Lin had destroyed to the tune of 21 million silver dollars;[49] (2) reopen Canton to foreign ships as well as the ports of Fuzhou, Ningbo, Xiamen (Amoy), and Shanghai; and (3) grant a lease to Britain of a tiny peninsula of thirty square miles named Hong Kong[50] (which the Portuguese had appropriately named *Os Ladrones*, "The Thieves"[51]). Sir Edward Belcher, the great-grandson of a governor of Massachusetts, raised the Union Jack on a small hillock called "Possession Point" on January

26, 1841 to take formal possession of England's Chinese colony, yet another jewel in Queen Victoria's crown.

Opium continued to flow into China, however, and by 1850 more than 50,000 chests entered the country.[52]

A significant footnote to Hong Kong's founding was the arrival of Sir Henry Pottinger and Admiral Sir William Parker in Macao aboard the steam-frigate *Sesostris*, which had come from London in a remarkably swift passage of sixty-seven days. The exceptionally rapid voyage of the *Sesostris* announced the impending victory of steam over sail, sounding the death knell of the tea clippers.

What with possession of a colony and the five-ports concessions, one might expect that the English increased their buying of China teas. But international politics are neither logical nor obvious, and the exact opposite occurred. Beginning with the Opium War, London tea merchants actually began to turn away from Chinese teas in favor of Indian teas. Ironically, it was Chinese tea plants taken to India that provided England's "Empire Tea."

The decade following the end of the Opium War was a terrible one for China. Natural disasters repeatedly struck between 1847 and 1849, causing widespread famine that culminated in a peasant's revolt (the Taiping Rebellion), which almost succeeded in overthrowing the Qing Dynasty. Adding to these woes was an invasion by the combined forces of the European powers in the Arrow War of 1856–1869. During this war British and French troops forced the Emperor to flee before they pillaged and burned the Summer Palace.

Like a hard nut that is difficult to crack, China was finally prized open and the bamboo curtain isolating it from the rest of the world for over a century was lifted. One of the few positive results of the Opium War was the interest it sparked in China. At this time many "China books" began to appear, which were eagerly snatched up in increasing numbers. The China books appealed especially to the Victorians, who were passionate readers of edifying armchair travel books, a way for every man to participate in the adventure of the Empire.

FORTUNE VISITS CHINA

Several European visitors to China wrote authoritative works that are still valid for reference. Among the better armchair travel books was the best-selling *Three Years Wanderings in the Northern Provinces of China*, published in 1848. Encouraged by this success the same author wrote a sequel in 1852 entitled *A Journey to the Tea Countries*. It was another best-seller. These informative books read like popular Late Victorian adventure fiction in the Henty vein. The author's name, Robert Fortune, seemed to have predestined him to perilous endeavors in the name of the Queen and the British Empire. A fearless, knowledgeable man, Fortune stated in the preface to *A Journey* that he had been "deputed by the Honourable the Court of Directors of the East India Company to proceed to China for the purpose of obtaining the finest varieties of the Tea-plant, as well as native manufacturers and implements, for the Government Tea plantations in the Himalayas."

Fortune disembarked in Hong Kong in 1848 and, traveling alone "disguised as a Chinaman, caring little for luxuries," he trekked to China's famous tea regions that were forbidden to foreigners.[53]

Fortune stated that the purpose of his book was to "give a peep into the Celestial Empire."[54] How understated this is. *A Journey* contains the best description of the cultivation, processing, preparation, and use of tea in China in the mid-nineteenth century. Since "Imperial Agent" Fortune wrote from firsthand experience, the factual basis and authentic aspect of his books make them even more reliable than Chinese sources of the period.

TEA CULTIVATION

China's immutability always surprises. Centuries-old traditions continue unchanged as if time had hardly advanced. The techniques used in the nineteenth century for the "generation" of tea plants by multiplication of tea seeds followed steps identical to those developed during the Tang Dynasty one thousand years earlier.

Tea seeds were collected in October and placed in a basket filled with a damp sand-earth mixture until March, when the sprouts were sown thickly in nursery beds. A year later planters waited until the spring rains before they transplanted the young tea plants in rows four feet apart with only five or six tea plants in each row.[55]

Large tea plantations were laid out along the flanks of hillsides, especially those facing north and east. Moongate entrances and doors of all Chinese houses faced the "Sacred South," but northeasterly exposures receiving the morning light were best for tea plants. Rainfall was another important consideration in choosing a new tea plantation because teamen never irrigated and terraced tea land was rare. Tea cultivated on elevations was termed "hill-tea" as opposed to "garden-tea" grown on level plains.

European visitors to China always commented that tea seemed to be cultivated everywhere. Indeed, tea plantations actually existed in every province save those producing rice and silk. Land there was too valuable to be used for tea.

Crops of millet and Indian corn introduced from America were sown
among garden-tea to provide the shade necessary to protect the young
plants in the hot summer months.[56] During cold winters straw was tied
around the bushes to insulate them from frost. All tea fields were constantly
weeded.

A one-year-old tea plant was between nine inches and one foot high. Its
branches were pruned only if necessary to form the bush. The first crop of
marketable tea leaves was picked after three years, when the tea bush had
attained its maximum height of from three to four feet. A mature bush eight
years old yielded an average of two to three pounds of tea annually for
many years, but a tea bush was considered old when it reached ten or
twelve years of age. At this time it was dug up and replaced by a young
tea plant, renewing the endless cycle practiced for centuries.

TEA MANUFACTURE

Europeans had mistakenly classified tea into two distinct species
because formerly it was believed that one species produced black tea and
another produced green tea. Nature and the Chinese ignore this differen-
tiation. Confusion probably arose because Chinese teamen rarely made
both black and green tea in the same district—except for Canton, where
European teamen working in European factories should have noticed the
obvious. As conclusive proof that processing and not genus determines
whether a tea is green or black, the famous black tea district Moning
once produced only green tea made with the same leaves from the same
trees.

China's tea was primarily grown in small, one-family gardens. Each
family harvested and processed the tea grown on their lands. This handicraft tea industry reached its height in the mid-1880s,[57] which were very
prosperous years for tea growers.[58] Needless to say, the vast number of
tea producers competing to produce fine teas kept the quality high and the
price low.

We have seen that the same fresh tea leaves could be made into either
black or green tea. Market economics certainly influenced which teas
were produced in each district, but these were not determinant. As in the
wine-growing regions of France, climate (cloud cover, mist, rainfall) and
soil (humus, minerals) added a qualitative extra to some tea, putting it
in a superior class apart from others. While the optimum growing
conditions in one region might favor the production of black tea, in
another the production of green tea was favored and regional specializa-
tion arose.

Black Tea Manufacture

To produce black tea the fresh, hand-picked tea leaves were withered on bamboo trays for between twelve to as many as eighteen hours, then the leaves were gathered up in handfuls and tossed into the air to separate them. They had become soft and flaccid during the withering and were left in piles to rest for at least one hour. At this stage the leaves emit a pleasant fragrance and begin to show a color change.

This resting period is actually a controlled fermentation and is the crucial step in the manufacture of black tea, which in reality has a reddish copper color. Next the leaves were placed in an iron pan and roasted for about five minutes before they were rolled and sieved. After another rest, again exposing the leaves to the air for about three hours, they were roasted three or four minutes, then rolled as before.

Roasting was the costliest step for the producers because of the scarcity (and resulting high price) of wood and charcoal. Wood fires had been used for the first roasting fires that gave an uneven heat, but for the final roasting charcoal fires were lighted that radiated a steady, even heat.

The leaves were dried over a low charcoal fire, then put into pans and warmed for a few minutes before another rolling and shaking-out onto bamboo trays. This process might be repeated several times until the leaves were perfectly twisted and dried. A final sifting separated the leaves according to size. This sorting determined the tea leaves' final grade.[59]

Green Tea Manufacture

Both green and black teas could be made from the same leaves, but the method of manufacture was different: Black teas were fermented while green teas were not.

Freshly picked tea leaves destined to become green tea were spread out thinly on bamboo trays and exposed to the air and sunlight for one or two hours, which was roughly the time it took to heat the roasting pans. A portion of leaves was put into each roasting pan and moved about rapidly with quick swirling motions of the hands, an action causing the leaves to "come alive in the pans, making a curious crackling noise as they became moist and flaccid while giving off steamy, fragrant vapors."[60] After four or five minutes the leaves were taken out and put on bamboo rolling tables attended by several muscular men who divided the leaves into little piles no bigger than what could be easily pressed into the hands. Each worker formed a ball with the leaves, rolling it on the bamboo table to compress it, which gave the leaves a twist. In large-scale manufactures the workers used their feet. Stripped almost naked because of the heat, workers supported themselves with their hands on a wooden crossbeam above their heads while with the soles of their dirty bare feet they tread on large canvas-covered balls containing the tea. The tea was compressed and shaped by the workers' weight and rolling.

The tea balls were then shaken out on flat trays but not allowed to rest (i.e., to ferment) since they were almost immediately put into roasting pans, where workers moved the leaves around rapidly with their hands. Often the leaves were rolled a second time.

The tea leaves dried after one or two hours and were a dull green that brightened later. At this point the color of the leaves was fixed and they could no longer be made into black tea.

In a final step the green tea leaves were passed through bamboo sieves and graded.[61]

TEA NOMENCLATURE

Depending on the complexity of production, different varieties and qualities of tea resulted. This necessitated a system of classification.

The Chinese have always had a passion for naming things, as a stroll through any Chinese garden aptly shows. Tea afforded them an excellent occasion to display their poetic naming talents; there are thousands of tea names. Chinese teas bore such flowery names as "First Spring Tea," "White Dew Tea," "Coral Dew Tea," "Dewy Shoots Tea," "Money Shoots Tea," or "Rivulet Gardens Tea."[62] Far too often people added a maximum of flourishes to attain truly absurd names: "Virgin's Passion of Ten-Thousand-Lakes-and-Mountains Spring-Moon Tea." Fantasy and lyrical consonance, as well as ideograms that were pleasing to Chinese eyes rather than reason, inspired the christening of many Chinese teas. Flowery names can be considered for what they are, merely pleasant brand names bearing absolutely no relation to any system of classification. Furthermore, the more flowery a name became, the more vague and meaningless it also became, trapping unwary tea-drinkers into buying low-grade teas.[63]

There was, however, a very logical system of tea classification. Since the earliest days of tea's history a classification system had existed. At first teas were classified by geographical origin; later, leaf size was added, then season of harvest, until finally in the Qing Dynasty the classification system burgeoned to include countless criteria spawning thousands of tea names that were precise in the extreme. The Manchu obsession with genealogy[64] no doubt exacerbated the classification problem as surely as the Imperial Tea Bureau, which employed thousands of eunuchs whose sole task was to organize and coordinate tea production and classify the vast amounts of tea produced all over the continent-country. Hundreds of varieties, kinds, sorts, classes, divisions, and subdivisions composed the Qing classification system, which resembled a monstrous Chinese puzzle. In the simplest system for classifying a tea there were four grades of leaf quality, two manufacturing quality grades, and 200 grades for place of origin.[65] A permutation shows the thousands upon thousands of possible grades a single tea could have.

The awesome Imperial Tea Bureau could have simplified the labelling madness but its bureaucrats were the worst abusers. Unbelievably, after the fall of the Qing Dynasty the Imperial Tea Bureau rumbled along on its own momentum, adding another one hundred new tea names.

Although the classification system of imperial days passed into history during the 1920s, it nonetheless left a heavy heritage. Today, despite a determined effort at simplification, the Chinese are still wrestling with an unwieldy tea classification system based on numbers.

Chinese tea classification remained a mystery to Western teamen, who used their own greatly abridged and simplified system of nomenclature. The spelling varied from language to language but generally a name of Chinese derivation designated the variety and quality of a tea—for example, the black teas Bohea, Congou, Souchong, Pekoe; and the green teas Singlo, Twankay, Hyson, Young Hyson, Hyson Skin, Imperial, and Gunpowder. This was the "tea Chinese" familiar to European and American tea-drinkers. Unfortunately, far too often inferior teas were given the name of famous teas or tea-growing regions, just one of the many fraudulent practices commonly perpetrated by unscrupulous dealers.

COLLATERAL TRADE

Collateral trades supplying the tea industry provided employment for thousands of specialized craftsmen. Making tea implements such as bamboo rolling-tables; seed, drying, and carrying baskets; and sieves provided year-round employment. Ambulating merchants selling these tea implements could enrich themselves sufficiently after a few years to set up a business in a large coastal city or provide their sons with private tutors in preparation for the Civil Service Exams.

Carpenters alone were paid high wages to meet the ever-increasing demand for more tea chests, as were the woodsmen who furnished the lumber. Porcelain potters especially were under constant pressure to increase production and maintain high levels of quality, while artists were asked to come up with superb new decorations for teaware.

TRANSPORTATION

Tea planting had been so extensive throughout China that Aeneas Anderson remarked, "tea seemed to cover all China." Except for rice and silk lands, tea was indeed cultivated everywhere, even on the outskirts of big cities although the best tea-growing regions were usually isolated and distant from any major market. An ancient proverb held that "Fine teas come from high mountains," and for centuries tea's romoteness, often inaccessibility, required a well-organized and efficient transportation system employing thousands of people to get tea to market.

Following the route taken by the renowned Bohea tea from the remote mountains where it grew to market provides an excellent example of the logistics and toil involved in transporting tea.

Thousands of small tea producers in the Bohea Mountains sent their ready-to-drink teas to Zongghihian, a large town of tea-*hongs*,[66] where all Bohea teas were refired and packed for re-expedition. Important dealers sampled and compared the season's teas, choosing those they liked that were mixed (teamen say "blended") with other teas until a *chop* had been put together. A *chop* (like so many words mistakenly thought to derive from Chinese, *chop* came from the Hindi word *châp*, meaning "stamp") consisted of roughly 620 to 630 tea chests. Each chest was branded with the Chinese ideogram chop marks used year after year to designate teas of a specific quality.

After the *chops* had been formed a great trek across the Bohea Mountains began. This mountainous tea highway was a trade route as impressive as the Great Trunk Route of India. Another Hindi word, *kulí* (rendered in English as "coolie") was given the porters carrying the tea chests. Each coolie carried either a single chest of fine tea or two chests of common teas.[67] The bamboo carrying rods were designed to allow chests of common teas to be set down upon the ground when the coolie rested, whereas chests of fine teas never touched the ground and were propped up in the air even when the coolie rested. Since an average of 700 to 800 *chops* (504,000 tea chests) were produced in the Bohea Mountains annually, tens of thousands of coolies were required just to carry them. Ant-like lines of coolies carrying precious loads of tea stretched along the narrow mountain paths for miles.[68]

Bohea Mountain coolies' work was a grueling toil. Trudging along with their heavy loads from early morning until nightfall, the coolies only stopped for hastily taken bowls of noodles and cups of sugared tea.[69]

A striking exception to the tea generally drunk in China was the strong, sickeningly sweet tea stirred with a special sugar-spoon drunk by the tea coolies. No one has yet pointed out that tea of this kind would be especially appreciated by opium addicts who had a perpetually parched throat and a craving for sweets. The work of the Bohea Mountain tea coolies was so cruelly arduous that it is not surprising they smoked opium and ate small, sticky black opium pills. Moreover, could they have accomplished their task without the painkilling opium?

The sickly waxen pallor; sunken, staring, black-rimmed eyes; sinewy oak-hard muscles; and brown bodies of the majority of coolies attest to the human toll exerted by the tea trade.

We have already discussed the economic interdependence of tea and opium, yet it is clear that drugging the coolies with opium proved necessary in order to transport the Bohea Mountain tea. The coolies' addiction was one of the controls the Chinese mandarins had over the tea trade, for if the British stopped furnishing opium the coolies, racked by the pain of withdrawal, could not have carried the tea out of the mountains and Europeans would have been deprived of the tea the Chinese believed they could "not live a day without."

Bullock trains certainly could have carried tons of tea more easily than men, and without involving opium. But why they were not used remained a riddle until 1938 when Anna Louise Strong, writing on the scarcity of food in nineteenth-century China in her remarkable book *One-Fifth of Mankind*, resolved the mystery. She made the astonishing observation, "The food supply has even conditioned transport. The narrow valley-lands of the South are too precious for grass so southern transport is . . . on the backs of human beings, who are *cheaper to feed than animals*."[70]

At night the coolies literally crammed into the small, dirty dormitory rooms erected for them along the way. There they slept on any available space on the floor without bedding or blankets.

Perhaps the fear of a severe beating (or the even worse punishment of having opium taken from them) inspired the coolies to never misplace or lose any of the tea chests. Outside each tea and noodle shop and each dormitory rested the loads of hundreds of coolies, yet even if all the tea chests looked alike a coolie had no difficulty recognizing his carrying poles.

After an exhausting six-day march the coolies deposited the tea chests in Hokow, a city of 300,000 inhabitants solely employed in the tea trade. Here were located the greatest Chinese tea-*hongs*, where wholesale tea dealers from all over China bought tea for their clients, including Europeans. Once they were sold, the tea chests were loaded onto canal boats that took the tea to all parts of the Celestial Empire and beyond. Altogether, from Bohea to Canton each tea chest traveled 1,190 miles.[71]

During transport great care had been taken to insure no tea was damaged, yet such care was taken only with fine teas and export teas. Common domestic teas were simply dumped into large baskets, carried willy-nilly from the mountains, and literally thrown into the holds of river barges.

At all times Imperial Tribute Teas had "great pains taken" in their production, transportation, and handling. The rare teas reserved for the Emperor's personal use were clipped off the bushes with golden scissors, wrapped carefully in yellow silk, put into locked lacquer tea chests, and then escorted to the Forbidden City by armed cavalry.

Normally six weeks were required for Bohea tea to reach Canton. But war, internal unrest, and frequent famines often disrupted tea transport, causing high stacks of tea to rot in the sun for lack of transport. Sometimes this destroyed an entire year's crop.

THE TEA MARKET

Money made by Chinese tea producers and transporters was a pittance compared to the great profits reaped by middlemen and mandarins. In the mid-nineteenth century the already low price of Chinese tea began to drop suddenly and the reduction hit the growers the hardest. Whereas a picul[72] of tea in 1846 had been worth between 20 and 30 taels,[73] in 1895 the same picul was worth only 10 taels, having lost half its value in half a century. What had happened to cause the dangerous price deflation? A glance at a few figures will prove most enlightening.

The total tea exports[74] for the following years were:

Years	Metric Tons
1879–1880	125,827
1889–1890	109,724
1899–1900	83,724
1909–1910	94,397
1919–1920	18,493
1921–1922	2,319
1922–1923	5,042

The figures[75] clearly show that Chinese tea exportations had dropped precipitously toward the end of the nineteenth century. Part of the reason lies with Chinese mandarins who decided to put less tea on the market, thereby hoping to bolster the price of Chinese tea. This policy failed miserably, as we have seen, because tea's price actually lost half its value. For this policy to have worked the Chinese needed a monopoly of the tea supply.[76]

Incredibly, the Chinese seem to have been the last to realize they had lost their tea monopoly. After 1839 the expression "All the tea in China" would need to be modified to "All the tea in China and in the British Empire." Robert Fortune alone had taken from China more than 20,000 tea plants, "a quantity of manufacturing implements," and "eight ex-perienced Chinese teamen" to the British East India Company's tea plantations in India.[77] Fortune was but one of the Company's imperial agents, and before him almost one million tea plants from China had been transplanted in India. Ceylon began producing tea as well in 1875. Loss of the tea monopoly meant that China could no longer impose tea's price on the world market.

England's advantage was China's disadvantage. The following table shows the dent English "Empire Tea" made in Chinese tea exports (in tons).[78]

Years	China	India	Ceylon
1888–1892	109,722	47,805	22,084
1908–1912	91,565	115,693	86,391
1924	34,000	155,000	88,000

Generally, the overall tea exportation of China fell from 54 percent in 1871 to 18 percent in 1898 and 11 percent in 1906.[79] The critical years were at the turn of the century. What events combined to ruin China's tea exports?

Going back 100 years to the late eighteenth century, it will be remem-bered that at that time smuggling and doctoring of tea had reached truly scandalous proportions decried largely when the shameful—and harm-ful—practices were exposed in Parliament. Despite the outrage no official action was taken in either England or America to protect tea-drinkers.

The root of the problem lay with the consumers themselves. Europeans and Americans expected their fine, expensive green teas to have a blue hue. As a sure sign of quality period tea guides recommended teas "blue as a sloe." Because Western tea-drinkers demanded it, European tea merchants requested that green Chinese export teas be dyed blue. Since the Chinese were not going to drink any of this tea they obligingly agreed to what in their minds must have seemed quite a singular request. The formula used during the Qing Dynasty to dye tea was to "crush Prussian

Blue to a fine powder and add gypsum in a ratio of three to four resulting
in a light blue dye powder. Add the dye powder five minutes before the
end of the last roasting."[80] Workmen whose hands had been stained a dark
blue spread the dye powder evenly over the leaves and turned them
constantly to insure uniform coloring.[81]

Dyeing the tea leaves improved their aspect, giving them the "lovely
look Europeans and Americans appreciated in high priced green China
teas."[82] The Chinese knew better than to drink such dyed teas, which
doctors at the time "estimated contained more than half a pound of plaster
and cyanide for every one hundred pounds of dyed tea consumed."[83] Had
the Europeans themselves not expressly requested dyed teas, one might
be tempted to suspect a sinister Chinese conspiracy to poison all the
long-nosed barbarians.

In addition to being dyed, these export-quality teas were scented with
Chloranthus and other scents to improve their aroma. China export-tea in
the nineteenth century was so artfully improved that one now wonders if
Europeans and Americans living then could have recognized the real thing.
Tea's artificial aspect and aroma easily masked adulterations such as the
addition of stones, tea dust, leaf sweepings, and even leaves from trees and
plants other than the tea plant.[84] In 1881 it was reported that "millions of
pounds of tea—doctored, rotten, and even tea that has already been
infused—was sent to the United States."[85]

Another widespread practice was to put a reputed chop mark on tea
chests containing inferior teas, a usage more dishonest than dangerous.[86]

By the end of the nineteenth century, however, both the British Parliament and the U.S. Congress had passed "Tea Acts" safeguarding purity,
quality, and "fitness for consumption." The Tea Acts themselves were long
overdue and certainly did provide needed protection, but the circumstances of their enactment raise some intriguing questions. Why had it taken
ages to pass protective legislation when conclusive proof of harmful
abuses had long existed? Why did the Tea Acts appear within a short time
from each other on both sides of the Atlantic? Why at that particular time?
Coincidence, while not impossible, is highly improbable. The legislators'
good faith should not be doubted, yet when the Tea Acts are viewed as part
of global politics they take on the unmistakable appearance of trade-war
arms sighting China's tea exports.

It is significant that when the Tea Acts became effective Englishmen
and Americans no longer depended on China for tea and had in fact turned
elsewhere.[87] Ever since Commodore Perry "opened up" Japan in 1857
Americans had imported the bulk of their green tea from there, while
Britain easily relied on her Empire for tea.[88]

Chinese teamen tried valiantly to hold on to their foreign tea markets. China's black *Qimum* (Keemum) tea from Anhui province was first made in the 1820s as English Breakfast Tea; by 1886 it had been overtaken by Assam tea sales and there was little the Chinese teamen could do to recover their lost market. In the same province a teaman named Yuan-Lung produced only green tea in the 1850s but as the market sagged for green tea he converted completely to making black tea.[89] Yet the Europeans wanted Empire Tea from India and not black China teas.

Britain had won the imperial tug-of-war with China, but now Russia posed the greatest threat to England's imperial designs. Again Chinese tea exports played a leading role in the imperial battle between Russia and England.

Queen Victoria incessantly warned of the "Russian menace" and Russian plans to invade British India. At one point she became so exasperated that she even threatened to abdicate, stating flatly, "If England is to kiss Russia's feet the Queen will not be a party to the humiliation of England and would lay down her crown. It is a question of Russian or British supremacy in the world."[90] The Empress-Queen's wise admonition was heard and heeded as England quietly went about weakening Czarist Russia, the only power posing a direct threat to England's virtual monopoly of the world's tea.

Since the signing of the Treaty of Nerchinsk on August 27, 1689, Chinese tea for Russian samovars traveled across the desert wastes by camel caravan (whence the name "Caravan tea" used for the smokey, black tea—Lapsang Souchong—favored by the Russians).[91] An average of eighteen long months was required for a one-way overland journey wrought with discomfort and danger. Caravan tea was very hard to get, therefore it was extremely expensive. It finally became so costly it could no longer be marketed and the centuries-old camel carvans came to a bankrupt end, forcing the Russians by buy their tea from English and German merchants. Then in 1903 the Transiberian Railway was completed. This railroad posed a tremendous threat to the British because the Russians could now easily send tea and other Chinese goods rapidly and cheaply to Europe directly by rail.[92] This greatly undercut the time and higher British costs of shipping Indian and Ceylonese teas by steamships through the new Suez Canal. By Russian rail the best Chinese teas, porcelain, and silk were linked directly to Moscow, Berlin, Paris, and the rest of Europe, arriving in perfect condition in just over a week.

Countless Russian merchants settled in China, outnumbering those of all other nationalities put together. Russian trade boomed. They built factories for the manufacture of brick tea, the first truly modern industrial manufacturing of tea in China.[93] The English and Americans, together controlling the world's sea lanes, all but abandoned the Chinese tea market.

For a little more than a decade Czarist Russia enjoyed a quasi-monopoly of the Chinese market, but such a time increment is a mere nothing in history. World War I and the Russian Revolution in 1917 occurring back-to-back caused a total rupture in Chino-Russian commercial relations, and overnight the Chinese lost their principal foreign customer.

Between the wars "English tea" eclipsed Chinese tea completely, and British Empire Tea during the 1930s was the Western world's most popular tea. China tea continued to be sold on the export market and was highly rated by tea lovers, but the number of tons exported was such a pale shadow of what it once had been that it seemed as if the Chinese tea exports had vanished.

With perfect logic and ample justification the Chinese could pass off the loss of foreign tea markets as of no consequence, which was the official attitude of the dying Qing Dynasty. Although a lack of tea exports worked disfavorably on China's balance of payments, it is wrong to think the Chinese tea market itself had suffered or disappeared. After all, they did possess the world's largest tea market. They alone could absorb the millions of pounds of tea produced annually in China. Although the total Chinese tea production has never been published, China's immense population drank an estimated four to seven pounds of tea per person annually. Multiplied by hundreds of millions, this meant that the total Chinese tea production for a single year exceeded 2 billion pounds if not more.

The loss of foreign tea markets did not affect Chinese tea manners or the pomp and circumstance of the Imperial Court. In 1912, the year the Qing Dynasty fell, no one in the Forbidden City could have presaged the coming cataclylsmic changes. Life rumbled on in feudal opulence.

A rare, amazing glimpse into the forbidden realm of the Emperor's presence was given by no less than China's last Emperor, Pu Yi (1906–1967), in his autobiography published in 1964. Tourists to Beijing can still see in the Forbidden City[94] the Emperor's personal "imperial yellow" porcelain teaware decorated with five-clawed dragons bearing the inscription "Ten Thousand Years of Eternal Life." No expense was spared to procure only the rarest, most costly porcelain teaware and rare teas for the august Son of Heaven who drank Imperial Tribute Teas grown in Forbidden Imperial Tea Groves.

Even the baroque extravagance of the Ottoman sultans pales beside the incomparable luxury and circumstance surrounding China's Emperor. "When I went into the Imperial Gardens an interminable procession followed me" related Emperor Pu Yi. Among the many Imperial Offices in the procession always trailing behind the Emperor were the "eunuchs of the Imperial Tea Bureau who carried an entire collection of boxes and chests containing a thousand kinds of biscuits, refreshments and sweets as well as an incalculable number of tea varieties, large pots of boiling water, and the necessary teaware."[95] All this for one person, a small child of six years of age, "in case I became thirsty."[96]

No one on earth could drink the Emperor's personal "forbidden teas" save a eunuch tea taster from the Imperial Tea Bureau who insured the Emperor's cup of tea had been properly brewed and a eunuch food taster who insured it contained no poison.

NOTES

1. P. Colquhoun, *A Treatise on the Wealth, Power, and Resources of the British Empire in Every Quarter of the World* (London: Joseph Mawman, 1815), Appendix, 26.

2. Ibid. The extent of smuggling is strikingly apparent when one compares import figures between 1771 and 1780. During this time 107 continental ships imported 118,783,118 lbs. of tea whereas the 79 authorized ships of the British East India Company imported 50,759,451 lbs. of tea.

3. Rudyard Kipling coined the phrase the "Great Game" in reference to the fight for the strategic northwest corner of India.

4. Joseph Jobé, ed., *Les grands voiliers du XVè au XIXè siècles* (Lausanne, Switzerland: Edita Lausanne, 1967), 191–204.

5. George Frederick Campbell, *China Tea Clippers* (London: Adland Coles, 1974), 1–38.

6. Fu Lo-Shu, *A Documentary Chronicle of Sino-Western Relations, 1644–1820* (Tucson: University of Arizona Press, 1966), 518–519, notes 83–84.

7. J. Rambosson, *Histoire et légendes des plantes utiles et curieuses* (Paris: Librairie de Firmin-Didot et Cie, Imprimeurs de l'Institut, 1881), 226.

8. J. Arthur Lower, *Ocean of Destiny* (Vancouver: University of British Columbia Press, 1978), 63.

9. Fu Lo-Shu, *Documentary Chronicle*, 161–164.

10. Philip Mason, *The Men Who Ruled India* (London: Jonathan Cape, 1985), 243.

11. Fu Lo-Shu, *Documentary Chronicle*, 578, note 448.

After the American Revolution broke out, Spain entered the war. The market for Spanish dollars was closed. From 1779–1785 no dollars were sent from London to Canton—the English coins were strictly forbidden to be exported by law—even after the peace was made. The English merchants at Canton, therefore, had dollar-shortage. They insisted that *hong* merchants accept their goods in exchange for their tea purchases, even though the Chinese *hong* merchants could not sell British goods because the demand was small.

12. Ibid., 519, note 87.
13. Colquhoun, *Treatise*, 48.

14. Bai Shouyi, ed., *An Outline History of China* (Beijing: Foreign Languages Press, 1982), 424. "Between 1781 and 1790 the total amount of tea shipped to England was valued at 96,267,833 *yuan* while England's exports of wool and spices to China amounted to 16,871,592 *yuan*, or roughly one-sixth the total of Chinese exports." One *yuan* is divided into one hundred cents, a dollar.

15. Saint-John de Crèvecoeur, *Lettres d'un cultivateur américain écrites à W. S. Écuyer*, vol. 2, ed. G. Bertier de Sauvigny (Paris: Slatkine Reprints, 1979), 194.

16. Fawn F. Brodie, *Thomas Jefferson: An Intimate History* (New York: W. W. Norton, 1974), chapter 32, note 41, page 465.

17. Honoré de Balzac, *La comédie humaine*, ed. Pierre Citron (Paris: Éditions du Seuil, 1966), 117.

18. Britain's George III, despite suffering from bouts of hereditary mental illness, showed sound judgement when he requested his physician, Sir George Baker, to bring him only "one of the opium pills" to relieve pain (Christopher Hibbert, *George IV* (London: Penguin Books, 1976), 107). His son and namesake George IV, on the other hand, had a lifelong drug problem. Beginning in 1781 there began almost daily reports of his "wild behavior" and "drunken brawls" in the Vauxhall and Ranelagh tea gardens from which he often had to be "dragged out." Even then laudanum was counteracting the purgatives he was frequently administered (108). He might display the "pomp and magnificence of a Persian satrap" at Carleton House but by 1806 his doctor, Sir Everard Howe, noted he was taking one hundred drops of laudanum every three hours (326–327). The "Oriental vice" incited his mother, Queen Caroline, to "write on the plain sheets of cheap paper which all the Royal Family at Windsor used" to caution him against "taking too much laudanum." The Queen should have heeded her own advice instead of doctoring herself with "dangerous amounts of laudanum and nervous medicines" and taking large doses of opium after being bled. George IV's brother, the Duke of Cumberland, was once remarked to have been in a "very nervous state owing to the large quantities of laudanum which he took" (361). Opiate abuse seems to have been a problem of the entire royal family. By 1820 the future George IV suffered from a "lameness in his hand," prompting Princess Charlotte to conclude, "large quantities of opium were liable to cause that" (385), while the Duke of Cumberland warned him that the amounts of drug he consumed would "kill him but previous to that, palsy him" (768). Thomas Jefferson also suffered a "lameness in the hand" said to have resulted from a fall in Paris. "Palsy in the hand" was a common result of habitual opiate abuse and can often be detected in a person's scribbled handwriting (Rambosson, *Histoire et légendes*, 229).

Laudanum was having less and less effect on Queen Victoria's uncle, who was known to spend "the greater part of the twenty-four hours in a state of stupor." Government ministers often found the monarch "incapacitated by laudanum" when they visited him to discuss state business. The Duke of Wellington, however, was surprised that after taking a dose of two hundred fifty drops of laudanum the king "remained quite capable of conducting a rational conversation." His lucidity may have been due to his "drinking the strongest iced tea to allay the internal heat," as Joseph Farington recorded. (Hibbert, *George IV*, 329. See *The Farington Diary by John Farington RA*, ed. James Greig, 18 vols. [London: Hutchinson, 1922–1928]). The King's ministers and Wellington were not medical men and can be excused for mistaking laudanum for the stronger opium, since it was reported in the very serious *Lancet* that the "medicines which have been administered for some time past have consisted chiefly of *ether* and the *sedative tincture of opium*" (773, italics in the original).

19. Mark Elvin, *The Pattern of the Chinese Past* (Stanford: Stanford University Press, 1973), 399.

20. Fu Lo-Shu, *Documentary Chronicle*, 381.

21. Rambosson, *Histoire et légendes*, 227–228.

22. Ibid., 233.

23. Robert Fortune, *A Journey to the Tea Countries of China* (London: John Murray, 1852), 289.

24. Christopher Hibbert, *The Great Mutiny, India 1857* (London: Penguin Books, 1986), 291. The actual phrase reads, "pitching into opium pills with a regularity that would have done credit to his father-in-law Thomas de Quincey."

25. Michael Greenberg, *British Trade and the Opening of China, 1800–1842* (Cambridge: Cambridge University Press, 1969), 3.

26. Ibid., 211. The use of the word "mob" so fashionable in the eighteenth century has been replaced by "turbulent masses" (*turba irata*) in sources from this period. Is this a reflection of the greater access of the middle classes to a classical education?

27. Lower, *Ocean*. The Pacific trade is treated in great detail here. Nootka Sound is a little bit north of Victoria Island in British Columbia.

28. Fu Lo-Shu, *Documentary Chronicle*, 580, note 458.

29. John M. Blum, ed., *The National Experience*, 3d ed. (New York: Harcourt, Brace, Jovanovich, 1973), 167–168. This action is commemorated in the marine hymn in the phrase "to the shores of Tripoli."

30. Fu Lo-Shu, *Documentary Chronicle*, 621, note 213.

31. Elvin, *Pattern*, 391.

32. Bai Shouyi, *Outline History*, 425. "In 1789 a total of 86 Western ships arrived in Canton, of which 61 were British and 15 were American. By 1832 62 American ships alone arrived in Canton." In 1839 on the eve of the outbreak of the Opium War the U.S. firm of Russell & Co. had no less than 1,500 chests of opium in its Canton factory compared to the 1,700 chests of the British Dent & Co. and the 7,000 chests of Jardine, Matheson.

33. Fu Lo-Shu, *Documentary Chronicle*, 622, note 220. John Quincy Adams had published in the *National Register* of 1818, No. 5, 139– 40, a letter condemning the opium traffic.

34. Ibid., 621, note 213.

35. George Orwell, *Essays and Journalism 1940–1943* (London: Book Club Associates, 1981), 526.

36. Bai Shouyi, *Outline History*, 436.

37. Greenberg, *British Trade*, 220. Greenberg has voiced the same opinion. He states that "during the years 1830–31 a total of $12,900,031 worth of opium was shipped to China." According to Greenberg, for these same years the opium shipments broke down to: Bengal, 5,672 chests; Malwa, 12,856 chests; Turkey, 1,428 chests; with a total of 19,956 chests. John Fairbank and Denis Twitchett in *Cambridge History of China*, vol. 2 (Cambridge: Cambridge University Press, 1980), 29 give the value of $1 as 0.72 taels.

38. Fu Lo-Shu, *Documentary Chronicle*, 380.

39. Bai Shouyi, *Outline History*, 431–435.

40. Ibid., 435. Bai Shouyi states that the opium confiscated by Imperial Commissioner Lin was "burned on Humen Beach."

41. Earl Swisher, *China's Management of the American Barbarians* (New York: Octagon Books, 1972), 81. Swisher points out that "Americans had no direct dealings with Commissioner Lin and there are only passing references to him in Sino-American documents." Lin had asked Mr. King of Olyphant & Co. to serve as a witness to the destruction of the confiscated opium.

42. Peter Lowe, *Britain in the Far East: A Survey from 1819 to the Present* (London: Longman, 1981), 13–14.

43. Fairbank and Twitchett, *Cambridge History*, 154.

44. Lowe, *Britain*, 14.

45. J. B. Sykes, ed., *Oxford English Dictionary* (Oxford: Clarendon Press, 1982), 1097.

46. Colquhoun, *Treatise*, 411.

47. Lowe, *Britain*, 15. Palmerston wrote Elliott, "I gave you specific demands and furnished you with the means of obtaining them. . . . You have disobeyed and neglected your instructions."

48. Swisher, *China's Management*, 8.

49. Bai Shouyi, *Outline History*, 435.

50. Andrew Boyle, ed., *Everyman's Encyclopaedia*, vol. 7 (London: J. M. Dent, 1909), 418. Britain appeared to have gotten an undesirable piece of property because the climate of Hong Kong was described as "unfavorable to Europeans owing to the rapid alternations of heat and cold, and the chief town [Victoria] retains the violent heat of the sun long after sunset, being hedged in by rocks which keep off the cool evening breezes." Britain's lease expires in 1997.

51. Fu Lo-Shu, *Documentary Chronicle*, 621, note 211.

52. Bai Shouyi, *Outline History*, 436.

53. Robert Fortune, *A Journey to the Tea Countries of China* (London: John Murray, 1852), Preface, v. Fortune declared, "No one seemed to have the slightest idea that I was a foreigner." Disguises in native costume became almost a cliché in nineteenth-century literature. MacKenzie had donned "native dress" as well when he went to the Bohea Hills, as had Sir Henry Pottinger and Captain John Christie during their secret mission to Persia and India.

54. Ibid., Preface, vi.

55. Ibid., 91.

56. In India tea gardens are protected from the sun by mature rubber trees. In some cases tea trees are allowed to mature, thus providing shade.

57. Fairbank and Twitchett, *Cambridge History*, 27. A remarkable short story written by the Frenchman Eugène Simon (who had been consul in Ningbo and Fuzhou in the 1860s) entitled *La famille Ouang-ming-tse* describes the life of a Chinese tea grower's family during the heyday of the handicraft tea industry.

58. Fortune, *Journey*, 580.

59. Ibid., 278–283.

60. Ibid., 277.

61. Ibid., 276–278.

62. Ibid., 271.

63. European tea names are not as flowery as Chinese tea names but they can be equally meaningless. A famous English tea purveyor commercializes a blend of Indian

and Ceylon teas named "Queen Anne Tea" although India and Ceylon (present-day Sri Lanka) did not produce tea until more than a century after Queen Anne's death. Another English tea purveyor offers black tea purported to be "like the tea of the Imperial Tang Dynasty," despite the lack of the least shred of evidence that black tea existed at the time of the Tang Dynasty.

64. Franz Michael, *The Origin of Manchu Rule in China* (New York: Octagon Books, 1972), 80–98. A clear, expert explanation of the Manchu clan element can be found here.

65. David Schapira, Joel Schapira, and Karl Schapira, *The Book of Coffee and Tea* (New York: St Martin's Press, 1975), 218.

66. Fortune, *Journey*, 202–203. On these pages are drawings of coolies carrying fine and common tea chests. In 1941 George Orwell could still comment, "We all live by robbing Asiatic coolies . . . and our standard of living demands that the robbery shall continue." *Collected Essays 1940–1943* (London: Book Club Associates, 1981), 581.

67. Ibid.

68. Ibid., 185.

69. Ibid., Chapters 11 and 15.

70. Anna Louise Strong, *One-Fifth of Mankind* (New York: Modern Age Books, 1938), 27 [italics added].

71. Sabine Yi, Jacques Jumeau-Lafond, and Michel Walsh, *Le livre de l'amateur du thé* (Paris: Robert Laffont, 1983), 90.

72. "Picul" derived from Malay *pikul*, meaning "to carry a heavy load." One picul = 133.33 lbs., or 60.477 kg.

73. "Tael" also derived from Malay and is equivalent to the Chinese measure *liang*, which is equal to 1/16 of a catty (1.1 lbs.) of silver. Thus, 1 tael = 1.1 oz.

74. Les Monographies de "La Dépêche Coloniale," *Les grands produits coloniaux: Le thé* (Paris: La Dépêche Coloniale Éditeur, 1926), 15.

75. The Chinese were most unreliable in publishing their export statistics. The U.S. Embassy furnished quite different figures of 26,015 metric tons in 1921 and 34,825 metric tons in 1922. The United States itself imported 7,000 metric tons of green tea in 1924, mostly from Japan. Corrected statistics reveal a peak export of 134,000 metric tons of China tea in 1886.

76. Fairbank and Twitchett, *Cambridge History*, 81. They have pointed out that "tea was China's most important export product until 1887 when silk overtook it."

77. Fortune, *Journey*, Preface, vi.

78. Les Monographies, *Les grands produits*, 15.

79. Fairbank and Twitchett, *Cambridge History*, 8.

80. Fortune, *Journey*, 94. Prussian blue is hydrated ferric ferrocyanide and gypsum is hydrated calcium sulfate, better known as plaster. Millions of Englishmen loved their "cuppa cha" and were not ready to give it up—even for the Empire. Imperial interests began to spread the rumor that China tea was unhealthy. See Appendix 1.

81. Ibid.

82. Ibid.

83. Ibid.

84. Ibid., 94.

85. Rambosson, *Histoire et légendes*, 316.

86. Fortune, *Journey*, 261.

gathering of friends and as many as possible would crowd onto the heated, raised brick platform (*kang*) upon which the family slept at night. The price of tea was high so each guest brought a small amount to contribute to the party. Some even brought their own *zhong* along as well. One of the host's children ran to a nearby teahouse to fetch some savory foods such as steamed buns, fried crisps, congees, and sweets to serve the guests.

Wood was scarce (therefore very expensive) in China. The cost of keeping a fire burning all day to boil tea water would be prohibitively high, so the Chinese invented the Shanxi tea stove. This was described by Anna Louise Strong in *One Fifth of Mankind* as a

> small portable clay stove held together by a framework of iron wire which served to heat tea water. Our host fed charcoal a piece at a time into a two-inch hole in the middle of the stove-top. Over the tiny flame a wide-bottomed but narrow-topped copper kettle was raised on three small stones just high enough to allow the fire to draw. The shape of the stove, of the kettle, and their relation to each other, had all been carefully adjusted to use every smallest bit of heat. In the summer the stove could easily be carried outdoors. (27–28)

Since tea parties cut across class lines they were not among the "evil practices of the bourgeoisie" the communists who came to power in 1949 wished to stamp out. Quite to the contrary, communist leaders embraced the tea party and those hosted weekly by Commissar Jou En-lai and Madame Sun Yat-sen for the foreign press corps became famous.[1]

TEAHOUSES

Receiving intimate friends for tea at home was one form of Chinese entertaining, but the real social life of China was found in the teahouses. Nothing better exemplifies the gregarious character of the Chinese than the teahouse. Omnipresent, vast numbers of teahouses lined the streets and parks of villages, towns, and cities. Often there were more teahouses than rice shops. Fortune remarked, "As usual in all the Chinese towns which I have visited, there were a vast number of tea and eating houses for the middle classes and the poor. They did not seem to lack customers for they were all crowded with hundreds of natives, who, for a few cash[2] can obtain a healthy and substantial meal."[3]

The countryside was also dotted with teahouses, picture perfect in the verdant landscape with graceful lilting eaves. Solitary teahouses tended by monks or hermits could be chanced upon in even the most isolated sites on remote mountains. No matter where they were located, a cup of tea always stood ready to welcome a stranger.

One entered the teahouse and chose any available chair at one of the lacquer tea tables. In winter the choice seats were near the stove, in summer near a window or door. Almost as soon as one had been seated a waiter materialized from nowhere to ask the traditional question, "What kind of tea would you like, Sir?" During the Qing Dynasty one could choose from an almost infinite variety of teas, requesting either a favorite name-tea or the house-tea. The waiter would place a *zhong* before the customer, put in a quantity of tea leaves, and fill it with boiling water. In general, tea was drunk "pure and genuine" (without milk or sugar) but in some regions it was customary to add sugar, and in other regions, milk. The waiter would refill the *zhong* with boiling water two or three times or until the strength and taste had been drawn out of the tea leaves.

In the larger teahouses musicians might play the *guanzi, pipa, erhu*, or *guqin* for background music. Singers were occasionally hired. Story telling, plays, and marionette shows were other popular forms of teahouse entertainment included in the very reasonable price of two *cash* per *zhong* of tea. Most people, however, went to the teahouses just to talk, rest, warm themselves by the fire, read, meditate, and play cards or majong.

Lao She said teahouses were frequented by "people from all walks of life and every possible character and persuasion. Teahouses were indeed a microcosm of Chinese society as a whole,"[4] where opium addicts, swindlers, card sharks, currency dealers, "come-on hostesses," and poets all rubbed shoulders. Order reigned among this hodge-podge of humanity because the cardinal rule observed in every teahouse was Hostility transformed to Hospitality. Harsh words or anger over tea were universally condemned and never forgotten.

Teahouse foods, infinite in variety, stressing quality rather than quantity, were generally steamed and served in multi-layer bamboo steamers. Chinese restaurants in the West, which are modeled after Chinese teahouses, are gradually adding the marvelous teahouse foods of China's imperial past to their menus. Usually these appear as appetizers known as the Cantonese *dim sum*, meaning literally to "dot the heart," or in Mandarin *dien xin*, the "heart-touchers,"—expressions that give an idea how savory teahouse foods can be. Steamed dumplings with meat stuffing, steamed meat balls, chicken salad with noodles, rice steamed in a lotus leaf, and spring rolls are among the many teahouse specialities. In addition there was an almost endless variety of fried crisps eaten with numerous delicious dips. In general, noodles replaced rice as the staple of teahouse meals, but people stopping in the teahouse for breakfast ate plain soft rice *congee* and tasty seasoned *congees* could be had throughout the day. People with a sweet tooth were well served by exquisite, inventive sweets and desserts in the teahouses.[5]

Anyone having spent time in Beijing is familiar with the fine yellow dust always in the air, dirt blown from the wastes of the Taklimakan Desert 2,000 miles away. Europeans living in the capital in the 1920s invented a dessert christened "Peking Dust" made of sweet powdered Longjiang chestnuts topped with cream, the only teahouse food of foreign origin.[6]

Teahouses naturally prepared dishes using tea. The most famous tea-house speciality dating as far back as the Song Dynasty and found in all Hangzhou teahouses was the marvelous dish of small freshwater shrimp from the West Lake cooked in the locally grown "Dragon Wells" (*Long-guing*) green tea.[7]

The last great period of teahouse glory was in the 1920s and 1930s. Europeans living in China preferred their restricted clubs where Chinese were unwelcome to the noisy teahouses frequented by the natives. Thus the Europeans missed the exuberant teahouse heyday that followed the Qing Dynasty's fall. Peek for a moment into China's lively teahouses and feel their special atmosphere described by Lao She:

> One could hear the most absurd stories . . . come into contact with the strangest views . . . hear the latest opera tune or the best way to prepare opium. In the teahouses one might also see rare art objects newly acquired by some patron—a jade fan pendant recently un-earthed or a three-color glazed snuff bottle. Yes the teahouse was indeed an important place; it could even be reckoned a kind of cultural center.[8]

Sadly, this was the last homage to the traditional teahouse. During the brutal Japanese occupation of China during World War II the teahouses were forced to close one after another as a thousand years of teahouse life was suddenly snuffed out.[9] Surviving teahouses had suffered irrevocably and their war wounds were glaring for all to see: "Everything from the building to the furniture was dull and shabby. Teahouse owners were obliged to take in lodgers to make ends meet."[10]

Refined teahouse foods became a fond memory, and lucky were the teahouses that could still offer salted melon seeds or peanuts. Credit formerly extended automatically to any client requesting it had gone and henceforth everyone, even steady customers, had to pay on the spot. Inflation was so bad that the cost of living sometimes doubled in a day; it became a standing joke that teahouse patrons had to pay in advance because the price of tea went up so fast its price increased as one drank it.[11] "Tea money" no longer kept teahouse owners in tea and many teahouses were closed in despair, their owners reduced to peddling hot tea in the streets after selling the teahouse that had been in their family for generations.[12]

The decades after 1949 were bleaker still, and the teahouses that had once flourished in such great numbers had practically vanished. Only in the late 1970s did a few authorized teahouses begin to show a timid comeback. Selected ruined teahouses were restored with care and re-opened on a trial basis. China's most famous teahouse in Shanghai built in the thirteenth century and now restored to pristine condition is a major tourist attraction. Music, classic ballads, and teahouse dramas are again infusing life and drawing crowds to the revitalized teahouses. Beijing-sponsored actors have even presented teahouse dramas in large European and U.S. cities in international cultural exchange programs. From the dismal brink of extinction teahouses have bounced back with surprising verve and once again show signs of regaining their former preeminence in China's social life.[13]

CHINA TEA TODAY

On the eve of World War II 20 million Chinese fled to safety in China's most fertile and most heavily populated province, "Four Rivers" Sichuan. Tea cultivation interrupted by the Japanese occupation was resumed with relatively little difficulty after the war as the experienced body of teamen sheltered in Sichuan returned to their homes and pre-war occupations.

After 1949 Chinese tea exports were erratic when they existed at all. The bamboo curtain then drawn across China led many Western tea-drinkers to mistakenly think of China's famous teas as legends, yet fortunately during this interlude China's tea production maintained proud levels of excellence.

Today, Chinese teas harvested between April 15 and May 15 are called the "First Crop."[14] The First Crop is the best quality China tea and the most abundant, accounting for roughly 55 percent of the year's harvest. At the beginning of summer the "Second Crop" is picked that represents good quality tea and thirty percent of the annual tea production. In some regions a "Third Crop" is harvested in the fall. Of middling quality, the Third Crop amounts nonetheless to 15 percent of all Chinese tea production. Each year more than 80 percent of all China tea is made into green tea.

The production and commercialization of tea, like all Chinese agricultural products, is a state monopoly. Government-owned provincial companies bearing the ponderous name "China National Native Produce and Animal By-Products Import and Export Corporation" (followed by the "Branch" telling the provincial capital and the "Office" listing the local producing city) are responsible for the manufacture and commercialization of each province's tea. Sea Dyke Brand China Fujian Oolong, for example, is Article Number AT 209—China National Native Produce and Animal By-Products Import and Export Corporation, Fujian Tea Branch, Xiamen Office. Only packages of China tea allow consumers to know with such precision the kind of tea they are drinking.

Unlike India, Sri Lanka, and African countries, whose teas bear individual garden names, Chinese teas are marketed by numbered Standards. Each Chinese Tea Branch and Tea Office ensures its teas conform year after year to a given Standard, the work of expert tea tasters like those working in the *hongs* of nineteenth-century China. Gunpowder Tea grades 1 to 4, for example, are numbered 9372, 9373, 9374, and 9375. A Gunpowder 9373 tastes like last year's 9373 and next year's 9373. Chinese Tea Standards are so trustworthy that its teas are the only ones in the world that can be bought without a prior sampling.[15] Furthermore, Chinese integrity is such that if a tea harvest is not up to the Tea Standard it will not be placed on the market that season.

Within the last decades a new generation of Asian and Western tea-drinkers have had the possibility of procuring celebrated Chinese teas. Fine (reputable) tea purveyors throughout the world can offer a discerning clientele Anhui *Qimen*, Huangshan *Maofen*, Qiyun *Guapian*, Zhejiang *Longjing*, Fujian *Wuyi Rock Tea*, "white tea" and other fine "champagne tea" *Oolongs* from Fujian and Taiwan, Sichuan *Erui*, Yunnan *Pu'er*, and Guizhou *Maojian*, plus a host of other fine China teas too numerous to list here. Many hold the best tea in the world comes from Sichuan's Lushan Botanic Garden, a preserved ancient tea grove formerly reserved for the Emperor's teas. This tea is named "Cloud Mist" and is reserved for visiting dignitaries to China.[16]

The Chinese are traditionally the greatest tea enthusiasts in the world. Tea in China is not only an ancient tradition, it is a way of life. Over a century ago Robert Fortune observed, "Tea is a Chinaman's favorite beverage from morning until night. Those acquainted with the habits of this people can scarcely conceive the idea of the Chinese existing were they deprived of the tea-plant."[17]

NOTES

1. T. H. White, "Chou En Lai," *Time* 112 (July 3, 1978): 140–142.

2. "The *cash* was a Chinese coin, thin and circular about 3/4 inch in diameter with a square hole in the middle for the convenience of stringing them. One string of cash equalled 1,000—the value of a *cash* = 1/1,000 of a tael or ounce of silver" (Earl Swisher, *China's Management of the American Barbarians* [New York: Octagon Books, 1972], 97, note 8).

3. Robert Fortune, *A Journey to the Tea Countries of China* (London: John Murray, 1852), 36.

4. Lao She, *Teahouse*, trans. John Howard-Gibbon (Beijing: Foreign Languages Press, 1980), 82.

5. There are so many mouth-watering books devoted to Chinese cooking that it is difficult to make a selection from them. I used Margaret Leeming and May Huang Man-hui, *Chinese Cooking* (London: Macdonald and Company, 1983); Lo Mei Hing, Giulia Marzotto Castorta, and Sun Tzi Hsi, *The Joy of Chinese Cooking* (New York: Crown, 1983); Kenneth Lo, *Chinese Food* (London: Cox and Wyman, 1974); Dan Gong, *Food and Drink in China* (Beijing: New World Press, 1986).

6. Lo, *Chinese Food*, 67.

7. Dan, *Food and Drink*, 72.

8. She, *Teahouse*, 5–6.

9. Peter Lowe, *Britain in the Far East: A Survey from 1819 to the Present* (London: Longman, 1981), 156–176.

10. She, *Teahouse*, 46.

11. Ibid., 50.

12. Ibid., 15.

13. "Life in the Middle Kingdom," *Time* 99 (February 21, 1972): 32–34. At the same time teahouses disappeared the tremendous opium problem in China was eradicated, which seems to indicate a correlation. Once again teahouses are open and again China is recognizing an increasing drug problem, especially in Yunnan province.

14. The word "crop" corresponds to "flush" used for India tea.

15. Sabine Yi, Jacques Jumeau-Lafond, and Michel Walsh, *Le livre de l'amateur du thé* (Paris: Robert Laffont, 1983), 141.

16. Ethne Clarke, *The Cup that Cheers* (London: Reader's Digest Association, 1983), 6. I wish to thank Mr. Sam Twining for his gift of this very interesting book to me. The question of the world's best tea makes an amusing debate but in the end the debate is vain, since the best tea in the world will be the tea that pleases a person best.

17. Fortune, *Journey*, 395.

Appendix A

Queen Victoria and China Tea

Official British foreign policy in the nineteenth century was embodied in Queen Victoria. Taking her role as Empress of India quite seriously, Victoria took Hindustani lessons and insisted that only Empire Tea from India be served at the royal tea tables. To the Bishop of London she stated in the distancing first person plural that so became her, "We get all our tea from India. We hope *you* get *your* tea from India as an encouragement to the Empire. We feel all should do so."

The nonplussed Bishop admitted he did not know where his tea came from, but admitted that he generally took green tea (from China), adding that he drank more of it than he should.

"That is a pity," intoned the Queen. "Too much green tea, we have heard, is quite dangerous. Tell Mrs. Temple [the Bishop's wife] that she shouldn't allow it," to which the Bishop retorted, "Mrs. Temple cannot interfere, Ma'am, I make it myself in my own study."

There were millions of Englishmen who, like the Bishop of London, would not give up their favorite beverage even after a rebuke by the Queen herself.

Source: Housman, L. *Victoria Regina*. Edinburgh: J. and J. Gray, 1949.

Appendix B

The Tea-Strength Fallacy

How strong is a cup of tea? Some people drink a cup of tea to go to sleep, others to keep awake. Some drink tea to calm their nerves, others for a lift. How can the same beverage possess such opposing qualities? Precisely because tea—unlike coffee—can produce both these effects upon the body, it is viewed as a wonder drink.

Tea and coffee both contain the stimulating substance caffeine, but only tea contains both caffeine and tannin. The presence of these chemical compounds together in tea leaves allows tea to act as a calming or exciting agent.

Here is how it works. Once boiling water is poured onto tea leaves, in the first two minutes all the caffeine in the leaves is drawn out. At this point tea is at its most stimulating. Only during the next minute will tannin gradually be drawn out of the tea leaves. This will not only cancel out the effects of the caffeine but after five minutes will actually make a relaxing, calming tea. Graphically it can be shown thus:

```
    Time
 ───────────────→
              Caffeine                Tannin
              Drawn-Out               Drawn-Out
  |_____|_____|

  ┌────────┬────────┬────────┬────────┬────────┐
  │  1st   │  2nd   │  3rd   │  4th   │  5th   │
  │ Minute │ Minute │ Minute │ Minute │ Minute │
  └────────┴────────┴────────┴────────┴────────┘

      |_____Stimulating____|_____Relaxing_____|
```

It becomes evident that the common notion of tea's strength is totally misconceived. The longer the tea leaves are allowed to infuse, the *less strength* (i.e., effective caffeine) it has.

Now one of the teaman's greatest secrets is out of the bag. There is no need to buy decaffeinated tea because anyone can decaffeinate a cup of tea. To do this simply boil a double amount of tea water. Infuse the tea leaves as usual for two minutes, then throw the infusion away. Pour the rest of the boiling water on the tea leaves and drink this brew after three minutes. It will be tasty and totally decaffeinated.

Green teas generally contain more caffeine than Oolong teas, which contain more caffeine than black teas. The reason for this lies in the processing the tea leaves undergo during manufacturing, because during fermentation much of the caffeine compounds are destroyed. The tea with the highest caffeine content is Gunpowder, which earned it the nickname "Gun-power." Put only a few pellets of this tea into a cup.

Again,

For a calming cup: Use less tea and longer (5 minutes) infusion time.

For a stimulating cup: Use more tea and shorter (2 minutes) infusion time.

Appendix C

Teaware

Primitive celadon had existed during the Shang Dynasty, but it was not until the Sui Dynasty in 589 that a discovery was made that would revolutionize ceramics. For the first time, a translucent white porcelain was invented. Objects made from this porcelain were lightweight and delicate yet shock resistant. Curiously, porcelain did not have the immediate popularity one would have expected; it only came into favor during the Ming Dynasty. There is a tendency to forget that the ancient Chinese did not use porcelain for drinking tea. Lacquer teaware has been found in Sichuan, and the archeological discovery at Mawangdui near Changsha shows that the Han were fond of elegant, eared *kouqi* cups. At this time it is clear that bowl-shaped cups in ceramic were made especially for tea as opposed to the *zun* used for wine goblets.

Throughout the history of tea ceramicware was made especially for tea-drinkers. As tea evolved there was a corresponding evolution in ceramics. Each period possessed characteristic teaware. White porcelain was a novelty in the Tang Dynasty but it was not commonly used. Preferred was ceramicware made with a white glaze, although tea lovers and especially tea purists such as Lu Yu recommended teaware that bore a light blue glaze thought to enhance the color of the tea infusion.

During the Song Dynasty powdered tea was in vogue; a special shallow bowl called a *qián* was made with a brown glaze called "rabbit's fur" or with a blue and light blue glaze.

During the Ming Dynasty ceramics reached a high degree of perfection. Pale green celadon is of unsurpassed beauty, but it was with porcelain that the Ming surpassed all other dynasties. Blue-and-white Ming porcelain was a commonly used teaware and it was this kind of teaware that seduced Europeans, who copied it in Delftware. Ming tea was drunk from a porcelain *zhong* consisting of a small, handleless cup covered with a matching lid and supported by a saucer.

At the beginning of the eighteenth century Europeans discovered the secret of making porcelain using kaolin and began to make excellent teaware. European porcelain manufacturers copied colors and motifs of Qing Dynasty teaware during a vogue for *chinoiserie*. Chinese export porcelain in the eighteenth century is known as *famille verte* (Green Family) and *famille rose* (Rose Family). Chinese porcelain from this period is marked with four to six ideograms indicating the dynasty, ruling emperor, and the year when it was made.

Today the variety of teaware on the market is truly astounding. As always, it is felt that the more beautiful the teaware, the better the tea will taste.

Appendix D

Tea Museums

China Trade Museum, Massachusetts
Hangzhou Tea Museum, Zhejiang Province, China
Hong Kong Tea Museum, Hong Kong
Tea Museum, Taipei, Taiwan
Victoria and Albert Museum, London (exhibition of "Tea Things")

Bibliography

SOURCES CITED

Books

Aleíjos. *T'u-Ch'uan, grüne Wunderdroge Tee*. 2d ed. Vienna: Wilhelm Braumülller, Universitäts-Verlagsbuchhandlung, GmbH., 1987.

Anderson, Aeneas. *Relation du voyage de Lord Macartney à la Chine*. Edited by Gilles Manceron. Paris: Éditions Aubier Montaigne, 1978.

Bai Shouyi, *An Outline History of China*. Beijing: Foreign Languages Press, 1982.

de Balzac, Honoré. *La comédie humaine*. Edited by Pierre Citron. Paris: Éditions du Seuil, 1966.

Behr, Edward. *Le dernier empereur: Pu Yi*. Paris: Éditions Robert Laffond, 1982.

Blofeld, John. *L'art chinois du thé*. Translated by Josette Herbert. Paris: Dervy-Livres, 1986.

Blum, John M., ed. *The National Experience*. 3d ed. New York: Harcourt, Brace, Jovanovich, 1973.

Boyle, Andrew, ed. *Everyman's Encyclopaedia*. London: J. M. Dent, 1909.

Brodie, Fawn F. *Thomas Jefferson: An Intimate History*. New York: Bantam Books, 1985.

Campbell, George Frederick. *China Tea Clippers*. London: Adland Coles, 1974.

Capon, Edward. *Tang China: Vision and Spendour of a Golden Age*. London: MacDonald Orbis, 1989.

Chatelain, E., and Quickerat, L. *Dictionnaire latin*. Paris: Hachette, 1891.

Chiang Fu-tsung. *Masterpieces of Chinese Portrait Painting in the National Palace Museum*. Taipei: National Palace Museum, 1971.

Clarke, Ethne. *The Cup that Cheers*. London: Reader's Digest Association, 1983.

Colquhoun, P. *A Treatise on the Wealth, Power, and Resources of the British Empire in Every Quarter of the World*. London: Joseph Mawman, 1815.

Coyle, L. Patrick. *The World Encyclopedia of Food*. London: Frances Pinter, 1982.

de Crèvecoeur, Saint-John. *Lettres d'un cultivateur américain écrites à W. S. Écuyer.* 2 vols. Edited by G. Bertier de Sauvigny. Paris: Slatkine Reprints, 1979.

Davis, W. S. *A Day in Old Rome.* Boston: Allyn and Bacon, 1950.

Dreyer, Edward L. *Early Ming China: A Political History, 1355–1435.* Stanford: Stanford University Press, 1982.

Elvin, Mark. *The Pattern of the Chinese Past.* Stanford: Stanford University Press, 1973.

Embree, Ainslie T., ed. *Encyclopedia of Asian History.* New York: Charles Scribner's Sons, 1988.

Fairbank, John King. *Trade and Diplomacy on the China Coast: The Opening of the Treaty Ports 1842–1854.* Stanford: Stanford University Press, 1969.

Fairbank, John K., and Twitchett, Denis, eds. *The Cambridge History of China.* Cambridge: Cambridge University Press, 1980.

Fitzgerald, Patrick. *Ancient China.* Oxford: Elsevier-Phaidon, 1978.

Fortune, Robert. *A Journey to the Tea Countries of China.* London: John Murray, 1852.

Fu Lo-Shu. *A Documentary Chronicle of Sino-Western Relations, 1644–1820.* Tucson: University of Arizona Press, 1966.

Gong, Dan. *Food and Drink in China.* Beijing: New World Press, 1986.

Greenburg, Michael. *British Trade and the Opening of China, 1800–1842.* Cambridge: Cambridge University Press, 1969.

Hammitzsch, Horst. *Zen in the Art of the Tea Ceremony.* New York: Avon Books, 1980.

Harler, C. R. *The Culture and Marketing of Tea.* London: Oxford University Press, 1964.

Herlin, Hans. *Das Taschenbuch vom Tee.* Munich: Wilhelm Heyne Verlag, 1980.

Hesse, Eelco. *Tee: Die Welt des Tees und die Tees der Welt.* 4th ed. Munich: Gräfe und Unzer, 1985.

Hibbert, Christopher. *Les empereurs de Chine.* Translated by Isabelle Reinharez. Paris: Éditions du Fanal, 1982.

———. *The Great Mutiny, India, 1857.* London: Allen Lane, 1978.

———. *George IV.* London: Penguin Books, 1976.

Hing, L. M.; Castorta, G. M.; and Hsi, S. T. *The Joy of Chinese Cooking.* New York: Crown 1983.

Hong Sheng. *The Palace of Eternal Youth.* Translated by Yang Xianyi and Gladys Yang. Beijing: Foreign Languages Press, 1982.

Jelínek, Jan, ed. *Illustrated Encyclopedia of Prehistoric Man.* Paris: Gründ, 1978.

Jenner, W.J.F. *Memories of Loyang.* Oxford: Clarendon Press, 1981.

Jobé, Joseph, ed. *Les grands voiliers du XVè au XXè siècles.* Lausanne, Switzerland: Edita Lausanne, 1967.

Jumeau-Lafond, Jacques. *Le thé.* Paris: Éditions Nathan, 1988.

Lacroix, Louis. *Les derniers grands voiliers.* Paris: Éditions Maritimes et d'Outre-Mer, 1974.

Lai, T. C. *At the Chinese Table.* Hong Kong: Oxford University Press, 1984.

Lamb, H. *Genghis Khan: Emperor of All Men.* New York: Bantam, 1953.

Lao She. *Teahouse.* Translated by John Howard-Gibbon. Beijing: Foreign Languages Press, 1980.

Leeming, M., and Huang Man-hui, M. *Chinese Cooking.* London: Macdonald and Company, 1983.

Lin Yutang. *The Importance of Living.* New York: John Day Company, 1937.

Lo, Kenneth. *Chinese Food.* London: Cox and Wyman, 1974.

Longford, Elizabeth. *Victoria R. I.* London: Weidenfield and Nicholson, 1964.

Lowe, Peter. *Britain in the Far East: A Survey from 1819 to the Present.* London: Longman, 1981.

Lower, J. Arthur. *Ocean of Destiny.* Vancouver: University of British Columbia Press, 1978.

Loyle, L. Patrick. *The World Encyclopedia of Food.* London: Frances Pinter, 1982.

Lu Hsun. *A Brief History of Chinese Fiction.* Translated by Yang Hsien-Yi and Gladys Yang. Beijing: Foreign Languages Press, 1982.

Lu Yu. *The Classic of Tea.* Translated by Francis Ross Carpenter. Boston: Little-Brown, 1974.

MacGregor, David R. *Tea Clippers: Their History and Development 1833–75.* Great Britain: Conway Maritime Press.

Maronde, Curt. *Heißgeliebter Tee.* Niedernhausen: Falken-Verlag, 1986.

———. *Rund um den Tee.* Frankfurt am Main: Fischer Taschenbuch Verlag GmbH., 1973.

Mason, Philip. *The Men Who Ruled India.* London: Jonathan Cape, 1985.

Michael, Franz. *The Origin of Manchu Rule in China.* New York: Octagon Books, 1972.

ter Molen, J. R. *Het goede leven Thee.* Utrecht/Antwerp: Het Spectrum, 1979.

Les Monographies de "La Dépêche Coloniale." *Les grands produits coloniaux: Le thé.* Paris: La Dépêche Coloniale Éditeur, 1926.

Nicolin, Marianne. *Tee für Genießer.* Niedernhausen: Falken-Verlag, 1982.

Orwell, George. *Essays and Journalism 1940–1943.* London: Book Club Associates, 1981.

Pu Yi. *J'étais empereur de Chine.* Translated by J. M. Gaillard-Paquet. Paris: Flammarion, 1975.

Rambosson, J. *Histoire et légendes des plantes utiles et curieuses.* 4th ed. Paris: Librairie de Firmin-Didot et Cie, Imprimeurs de l'Institut, 1881.

Runner, Jean. *Le thé.* 2d ed. Paris: Presses Universitaires de France, 1974.

Ruske, Sonja. *Tee.* Niedernhausen: Falken-Verlag, 1980.

Schapira, David; Schapira, Joel; and Schapira, Karl. *The Book of Coffee and Tea.* New York: St Martin's Press, 1975.

Schiaffino, Mariarosa. *L'heure du thé.* Paris: Gentleman Éditeur, 1987.

de Sélincourt, A. *Arrian's Campaigns of Alexander.* London: Penguin Classics, 1971.

Seneca, M. Annaeus. *Epistulae ad Lucilium.* Edited by R. M. Grammere. Cambridge, MA: Loeb Classical Library, Harvard University Press, 1958.

Serruys, Father Henry. *The Mongols and Ming China: Customs and History.* London: Variorum Reprints, 1987.

Strachey, Lytton. *Queen Victoria.* London: Guild Publishing, 1988.

Svensson, Sam. ed. *Les grands voiliers.* Switzerland: Hatier, 1984.

Swisher, Earl. *China's Management of the American Barbarians.* New York: Octagon Books, 1972.

Sykes, J. B., ed. *Oxford English Dictionary.* Oxford: Clarendon Press, 1982.

Tang Xianzu. *Peony Pavilion (Mudan Ting).* Translated by Cyril Birch. Bloomington: Indiana University Press, 1980.

"Tea Importation Act and Regulations." *United States Code—Code of Federal Regulations and Federal Register.* March 2, 1897/May 16, 1908/May 31, 1920 (Washington, D.C.: U.S. Government Printing Office.

Timkovski, M. G. *Voyage à Pékin en 1820–1831*. Paris: Librairie Orientale de Dondey-Dupré Père et Fils, 1827.

Tsao Hsueh-chin. *A Dream of Red Mansions*. Translated by Yang Hsien-Yi and Gladys Yang. Beijing: Foreign Languages Press, 1978.

T'Serstevens, A. *Le livre de Marco Polo.* Paris: Éditions Albin Michel, 1955.

Twitchett, Denis, and Wright, Arthur F., eds. *Perspectives on the T'ang.* New Haven: Yale University Press, 1973.

Ubenauf, Inge. *Vom höchsten Genuß des Teetrinkers*. Niedernhausen: Falken-Verlag, 1983.

van Gulik, Robert H. *Sexual Life in Ancient China*. Leiden: E. J. Brill, 1974.

Vollner, John E., Keall, E. J., and Nagai-Berthrong, E. *Silk Roads, China Ships: An Exhibition of East-West Trade*. Toronto: Royal Ontario Museum, 1983.

Wagner, Richard. *Parsifal*. Stuttgart: Philipp Reclam, 1980.

Wou Tche-he. *L'art du thé*. Translated by Nadine Normand. Taiwan: Éditions Philippe-Picquier, 1990.

Wu Cheng'en. *Journey to the West*. 3 vols. Beijing: Foreign Languages Press, 1982.

Wu Ching-tzu. *The Scholars*. Translated by Yang Hsien-Yi and Gladys Yang. Beijing: Foreign Languages Press, 1983.

Yi, Sabine; Jumeau-Lafond, Jacques; and Walsh, Michel. *Le livre de l'amateur du thé*. Paris: Robert Laffont, 1983.

Zhang Binglun. *Ancient China's Technology and Science*. Beijing: Chinese Academy of Sciences, 1983.

Zhou Chen Cong. *On Chinese Gardens*. Shanghai: Tongji University Press, 1984.

Articles

"Life in the Middle Kingdom." *Time* 99 (February 21, 1972).

"Super Tomb, Ch'in Shih Huang Ti." *Scientific American* 233 (September 1975).

"Chih Shih-huang Ti Find." *Science Digest* 78 (October 1975).

"Tea as Medicine." *Science Digest* 69 (June 1971).

Bosley, Galen C. "Caffeine: Is It So Harmless?" *Ministry Magazine* (August 1986).

White, T. H. "Chou En Lai." *Time* 112 (July 3, 1978).

SOURCES CONSULTED

Abel, Armand, ed. *La Chine et l'Extrême Orient*. Brussels: Meddons, 1970.

Alley, Rewi, and Burchett, Wilfred Graham. *La Chine, une autre qualité de vie*. Paris: F. Maspero, 1975.

Backus, Charles. *The Nan-chao Kingdom and T'ang China's Southwestern Frontier*. Cambridge: Cambridge University Press, 1981.

Bagley, Robert, ed. *Catalog: Treasures of the Bronze Age of China*. Exhibition at the Metropolitan Museum of Art, New York, April 12–July 9, 1980. New York: Metropolitan Museum of Art, 1980.

Balazs, Étienne. *La bureaucratie céleste*. Paris: Gallimard, 1968.

Behr, Edward. *Le dernier empereur*. Paris: Éditions Robert Laffond, 1982.

Bence-Jones, Mark. *Clive of India*. London: Constable, 1974.

Bingham, Woodbridge. *The Founding of the T'ang Dynasty*. New York: Octagon Books, 1975.

Boxer, C. R. *Portuguese Conquest and Commerce in Southern Asia, 1500–1750*. London: Variorum Reprints, 1985.

Buchanan, Keith; Fitzgerald, Charles Patrick; and Ronan, Colin Allistair. *La Chine éternelle: Le passé et le présent*. Paris: Nathan, 1981.

Chen Heyi; Tsian, Hao; and Ron, Souitchou. *Des profondeurs de la terre chinoise*. Paris: Cercle d'Art, 1982.

Chen, Vincent. *Sino-Russian Relations in the Seventeenth Century*. The Hague: Martinus Nijhoff, 1966.

Commeaux, Charles. *La vie quotidienne en Chine sous les Manchous*. Paris: Librairie Hachette, 1970.

Dawood, Nawaz. *Tea and Poverty*. Hong Kong: Urban Rural Mission—Christian Conference of Asia, 1980.

Delahaye, Hubert, and Han Zhongmin. *La Chine: 5,000 ans d'histoire et d'archéologie*. Paris: Belfond, 1985.

Dun, J. L., ed. *The Essence of Chinese Civilization*. New York: Van Nostrand, 1967.

Eden, Thomas. *Tea*. 3d. ed. London: Longman, 1976.

Elisseff, Danielle, and Eliseev, Vadim. *La civilisation de la Chine classique*. Paris: Arthaud, 1979.

Elvin, Mark. *The Pattern of the Chinese Past*. Stanford: Stanford University Press, 1973.

Escarra, Jean. *La Chine passé et présent*. Paris: A. Colin, 1937.

Feuerwerker, Albert. *State and Society in 18th Century China—The Ch'ing Empire in Its Glory*. Ann Arbor: Michigan Center for Chinese Studies, 1976.

Food and Agriculture Organization. *Tea Processing*. Rome: FAO, 1974.

Fossati, George. *Chine*. Preface by Anthony Burgess. Paris: Nathan, 1983.

Fronty, Laura. *Boissons aromatisées et tisanes*. Paris: Solar, 1983.

Gaubil, le Père Antoine. *Correspondence de Pékin 1722–1759*. Geneva: Librairie Droz, 1970.

Gentelle, Pierre. *L'etat de la Chine*. Paris: Le Découverte, 1989.

——— . *Chine, un atlas économique*. Paris: Fayard/Reclus, 1987.

Gernet, Jacques. *Le monde chinois*. Paris: Armand Colin, 1972.

Goepper, Roger, ed. *La Chine ancienne*. Paris: Bordas, 1988.

Gravereau, Jacques. *La Chine après l'utopie*. Paris: Berger-Levrault, 1983.

Griffin, Keith. *Institutional Reform and Economic Development in the Chinese Countryside*. London: Macmillan, 1984.

Grosier, Jean-Baptiste. *Les Chinois*. Paris: Solar, 1981.

Grousset, René. *La Chine*. Paris: G. Crès, 1930.

Herlin, Hans. *Das Taschenbuch vom Tee*. Munich: Wilhelm Heyne Verlag, 1980.

Huard, Pierre, and Wong Ming. *Chine d'hier et d'aujourd'hui*. Paris: Horizons de France, 1972.

de Kermadec, Jean-Michel. *Les paradoxes de la Chine*. Paris: Encre, 1989.

Ku Pan. *Courtier and Commoner in Ancient China*. Translated by Burton Watson. New York: Columbia University Press, 1974.

Lamour, C., and Lamberti, M. *Les grandes manoeuvres de l'opium*. Paris: Seuil, 1972.

Langlois, John C., ed. *China under Mongol Rule*. Princeton: Princeton University Press, 1981.

Lin Jung-en. *Six Yüan Plays*. London: Penguin Books, 1972.

Lin Yutang. *La Chine et les chinois*. Preface by Pearl S. Buck. Paris: Payot, 1937.

Mancall, Mark. *China at the Center: 300 Years of Foreign Policy*. London: Collier Macmillan, 1984.

March, Andrew. *The Idea of China: Myth and Theory in Geographic Thought*. Newton Abbot, England: David and Charles, 1974.

Marchisio, Hélène. *La vie dans les campagnes chinoises*. Paris: Édition du Centurion, 1982.

Martin, François. *Mémoires sur l'établissement des colonies françaises aux Indes orientales*. Paris: V. Giard, 1931.

Misra, S. R. *Tea Industry in India*. India: Ashish Publishing House, 1985.

Mo, Timothy. *An Insular Possession*. London: Picador, 1986.

Needham, Joseph. *Science and Civilization in China*. 4 vols. Cambridge: Cambridge University Press, 1971–1986.

Okakura, Kakuzo. *Le livre du thé*. Translated by Gabriel Mourey. Paris: André Delpeuch Éditeur, 1927.

Olivier-Lacamp, Max. *Les deux Asies*. Paris: Bernard Grasset, 1966.

O'Neill, Hugh B. *Companion to Chinese History*. New York: Facts on File Publications, 1987.

Parish, William, and Whyte, Martin. *Village and Family in Contemporary China*. Chicago: University of Chicago Press, 1978.

Perkins, Dwight, and Yusul, Shakid. *Rural Development in China*. Baltimore: Johns Hopkins University Press, 1984.

Pimpaneau, Jacques. *La Chine, culture et traditions*. Arles: Philippe Picquier, 1988.

Pinto, Fernão Mendes. *La pérégrination: La Chine et le Japon au XVIè siècle vu par un portugais*. Paris: Calmann-Lévy, 1968.

Pirazzoli-t'Serstevens, Michèle. *La civilisation du royaume de Dian à l'époque Han*. Paris: École d'Extrême Orient, 1974.

The Population Atlas of China. Hong Kong: Oxford University Press, 1987.

Qu Tong Zu. *Han Social Structure*. Edited by J. L. Dull. Seattle: University of Washington Press, 1972.

Ricci, le Père Matthieu. *Histoire de l'expédition chrétienne au royaume de la Chine 1582–1610*. Paris: Desclée de Brouwer, 1978.

Roi, Jacques. *Traité des plantes médicinales chinoises*. Paris: Éditions Paul Lechevalier, 1955.

Scheibenpflug, Lotte. *Das kleine Buch vom Tee*. Innsbruck: Pinguin-Verlag, 1977.

Schurmann, Herbert Franz, trans. *Economic Structure of the Yüan Dynasty*. Cambridge, MA: Harvard University Press, 1967.

Sen, Shoshitsu. *Le Zen et le thé*. Paris: Jean-Cyrille Godefroy, 1987.

Smith, Arthur H. *Village Life in China: A Study in Sociology*. New York: F. H. Revell, 1899.

Snow, Helen Foster. *My China Years*. London: Harrap Ltd., 1984.

Spear, Percival. *Master of Bengal: Clive and His India*. London: Thames and Hudson, 1975.

Sullivan, Michael. *Chinese Art: Recent Discoveries*. London: Thames and Hudson, 1973.

Swisher, Earl. *China's Management of the American Barbarians*. New York: Octagon Books, 1972.

Temple, Robert. *Quand la Chine nous précédait*. Preface by Joseph Needham. Paris: Bordas, 1987.

Toynbee, Arnold, ed. *La Chine d' hier à aujourd' hui*. Paris: Bordas, 1981.

Ukers, William H. *The Romance of Tea*. New York: The Tea and Coffee Trade Journal Co., 1936.

UNESCO. *La Chine: Passé et présent*. Paris: UNESCO, 1985.

Unschuld, Darel U. *Medicine in China*. Berkeley: University of California Press, 1986.

Vandermeersch, Léon. *Le nouveau monde sinisé*. Paris: Presse Universitaire de France, 1986.

Wang Gungwu. *The Structure of Power in North China during the Five Dynasties*. Stanford: Stanford University Press, 1963.

Watson, William. *Ancient China*. London: British Broadcasting Corporation, 1974.

———. *China before the Han Dynasty*. London: Thames and Hudson, 1961.

Whitney, Clara. *Clara's Diary, An American Girl in Meiji Japan*. Tokyo: Kodansha International, 1978.

Wu Wen, ed. *La Chine et ses trésors*. Paris: Comité d'organisation chargé de l'exposition des découvertes archéologiques de la République Populaire de Chine, 1973.

Index

ABOUT THE AUTHOR

JOHN C. EVANS is an independent researcher currently living in Paris. He has written on ancient and medieval European topics, and is presently involved in research on teahouses and tea in Japan.